YOUR MENTAL HEALTH RECOVERY WORKBOOK

TRIGGER™

The mental health & wellbeing publisher

ENDORSEMENTS

"Katherine has distilled many of the important lessons she has learned from and about living with a serious mental illness over the previous two decades. Combining her own life experiences with valuable techniques, she offers the reader a near-exhaustive array of strategies for making the most of their daily life challenges, whether or not they have to do directly with mental illness or the stigma associated with it. Limiting each topic to one page enables readers to go at their own pace and to pick and choose the topics or challenges most relevant for them at any given time without feeling overburdened or overwhelmed. This is a tour de force not only for anyone living with a mental illness and their loved ones, but for those who feel in the need for some practical, down-to-earth guidance on how to make the most of life."

> – Larry Davidson, PhD, Professor of Psychiatry, Program for Recovery and Community Health, School of Medicine, Yale University

"Katherine Ponte's recovery work lays out the principles and practices that help people in their recovery experience. It is full of skills which workbook participants might try as they consider their priorities. Katherine comes at this from two perspectives: as a person with lived experience AND as a thought leader in the recovery space."

> – Patrick Corrigan, PsyD, Distinguished Professor of Psychology, Illinois Institute of Technology, Director, Center for Health Equity, Education and Research

"Katherine Ponte's workbook offers patients who struggle with significant mental health conditions a road map to freedom. It guides them to discover the path toward a greater quality of life and ways to rise above the limitations and sense of stigma otherwise imposed by the burden of serious mental illness. Her writing is refreshingly clear, direct and straightforward. Readers cannot help but feel a sense of empowerment and personal competency attainable from mastering the skills and strategies she describes. Clinicians will find this to be a useful adjunct in their work with patients striving toward mental health recovery. Caregivers will feel a sense of relief and clarity about how they can render better support to their loved ones while simultaneously maintaining their own self-care. Katherine brings unsurpassed credibility from the worlds of both personal lived experience and scholarly study of the recovery process."

> – Joseph F. Goldberg, MD, Clinical Professor of Psychiatry, Icahn School of Medicine at Mount Sinai

"As a psychiatric occupational therapist working with people with serious mental illness for over 35 years, I can attest that this workbook is an outstanding tool in helping patients on the path to mental health recovery. The workbook is a treasure trove of best practices. In a direct and supportive manner, Katherine provides evidence-based steps for the reader using a caring and warm approach. The easily accessible information helps individuals navigate the mental health system while bridging the gap to participation in the wider community. I look forward to using it with my patients in the future."

> – E. Chaya Weinstein, PhD, OTR/L, Mental Health Recovery Occupational Therapy (OT)

"As a parent of someone living with serious mental illness (SMI), I found Katherine Ponte's workbook invaluable. The number one goal for those who support loved ones with SMI needs to be to protect the relationship. This workbook provides a wealth of opportunities for improving family outcomes by encouraging conversations based on the lived experience of the person in recovery. In my family, it opened up discussions about the loneliness and isolation of living with SMI. It led to simple and concrete solutions to everyday problems. It also helps the individual communicate more clearly about their symptoms and needs. I highly recommend it, both for people living with mental illness and for those who love them."

> – John DeNatale, National Alliance on Mental Illness-NYC Board Member and Family-to-Family facilitator

YOUR MENTAL HEALTH RECOVERY WORKBOOK

A WORKBOOK
TO SHARE HOPE

Katherine Ponte, BA, JD, MBA, CPRP
Founder, ForLikeMinds
Faculty, Program for Recovery and
Community Health,
Department of Psychiatry,
School of Medicine,
Yale University

Published in 2023 by Trigger Publishing
An imprint of Shaw Callaghan Ltd
UK Office
The Stanley Building
7 Pancras Square
Kings Cross
London N1C 4AG

US Office
On Point Executive Center, Inc
3030 N Rocky Point Drive W
Suite 150
Tampa, FL 33607
www.triggerhub.org

A CIP catalogue record for this book is available upon request from the British Library
ISBN: 9781837969975
Ebook ISBN: 9781837962426

DEDICATION

A journey of recovery is best traveled in the company of supportive loved ones, friends and providers. I have a few special ones to thank.

Izzy, my caring spouse, for all of his love and support during both the hard times and the good times.

Chaya, my kind hospital occupational therapist, for connecting me with peers who inspired me.

Dr. Goldberg, my amazing psychiatrist, for showing me there is always reason to hope.

Dr. Davidson, my wonderful mentor, for showing me that my lived experience matters and can help others.

ABOUT THE AUTHOR

Katherine Ponte, BA, JD, MBA, CPRP is a mental health recovery advocate, published author, non-profit founder, entrepreneur, coach and lawyer. She is a Certified Psychiatric Rehabilitation Practitioner and faculty member of the Department of Psychiatry's Program for Recovery and Community Health at Yale University. She built the ForLikeMinds platform of recovery-focused mental health initiatives and its associated community of over 100,000 that has reached millions. She is on the board of the National Alliance on Mental Illness-NYC. Katherine has lived with severe bipolar I disorder with psychosis for over 20 years and has been happily living in recovery since 2018. She is based in New York, USA.

CONTENTS

CONTENTS

Mental illness can evolve through many stages. Like when a caterpillar turns into a butterfly, an old life may seem to end in isolation, but can be transformed almost magically into something more beautiful. This beauty is recovery, and the magic is hope.

—Katherine Ponte

UNDERSTANDING MENTAL HEALTH RECOVERY

For too long, I didn't appreciate the complexities of the journey of mental illness, with its different stages of challenge through to recovery.

I was conditioned to view my illness on a scale of "bad" or "severe" to "less bad" and "less severe." There was no thought of moving *beyond* that range of "badness." There was no sense of progress over time. I was accustomed to doctors describing my condition based on how I was doing *at that moment* rather than where I was on any kind of mental health *journey*.

To me, this experience echoes the core of what's wrong with the way mental illness is generally approached – as a *permanent* state rather than as a potential *path toward living well*. In fact, I wasn't even aware of the prospect of "recovery" until my third and last hospitalization for mental illness.

Only when I started feeling better after making proactive changes in my *own* care after that hospitalization, did I have the life-changing realization that mental illness really is a *process* in which we, the "patients," can play an active role.

And it is my strong belief that approaching it this way – as a process and a journey *to recovery* – can not only foster hope and improve treatment outcomes but also help loved ones understand and participate in the recovery experience.

This concept of living "in recovery" with a mental illness might be foreign to you. Like me, you may have been given the impression that your illness is for life, with little mention ever having been made of living *well*. My hope is that this workbook will ignite in you a new mindset – of hope, recovery and optimal health.

THE CONCEPT OF RECOVERY

As I took more ownership of my care after my third hospitalization – and, in so doing, became a *student* of mental illness – I learned that there is significant research and evidence to support the concept of "recovery". Much of this research supports a more *constructive* understanding of both the possibilities and stages of living with mental illness.

The recovery experience was described by William A. Anthony, a leading scholar in the early days of mental health recovery research, as:

> "… A deeply personal, unique process of changing one's attitudes, values, feelings, goals, skills and/or roles. It is a way of living a satisfying, hopeful and contributing life even with limitations caused by illness. Recovery involves the development of new meaning and purpose in one's life as one grows beyond the catastrophic effects of mental illness" (Anthony, 1993).

Many people define recovery as being able to enjoy a combination of meaningful work, healthy relationships and community involvement while living with mental illness.

Do note, however, that when we talk about recovery, it is still important to acknowledge that it means living *with* a mental illness. Recovery does not suggest that the illness has vanished or been "cured." It simply pertains to the quality of life you are experiencing and the potential to experience life at its fullest, *alongside* your mental illness.

WHAT DO WE MEAN BY "MENTAL ILLNESS"?

There are many different types of serious mental illness – also often referred to as SMIs. These are largely defined by their impact on one's ability to function in typical daily activities.

The National Institute of Mental Health, part of the US Department of Health and Human Services (National Institute of Mental Health, n.d.), defines an SMI as a "mental, behavioral or emotional disorder resulting in serious functional impairment, which substantially interferes with or limits one or more major life activities." Illnesses considered SMIs primarily include bipolar disorder, major depressive disorder, schizophrenia and schizoaffective disorder. Please note, however, that this workbook is not limited to these illnesses. The emphasis *here* is on whether your mental illness substantially *interferes* with your life. Therefore, a serious mental illness – and one from which you will want to work toward recovery – may also include conditions such as anxiety disorders, eating disorders, personality disorders and beyond. The point is that we are not confined to a list of illnesses, but rather we are committed to considering and trying to improve our experience of them.

MENTAL HEALTH AS A JOURNEY

It's important to emphasize that there are many stages in the mental health journey, they're not always clearly defined, and everyone's journey, and the way they view the stages of it, is unique. These stages will also likely overlap. Like those of many, my path to recovery was not linear.

I have come to view the stages in my *own* mental health journey in terms of the following stages, through which I have moved forward and often backward and forward again:

- Symptom onset and diagnosis
- Crisis
- Withdrawal and isolation
- Treatment
- Relapse
- Stability
- Remission
- Recovery

But *your* experience, and the language that you assign to it, will depend on individual circumstances beyond just your specific mental health condition, including how big a role your loved ones and other supporters play in your journey, and how much access to professional mental health *care* you have.

Having said this, there are still many commonalities across individual experiences with mental illness, with perhaps the most important being the possibility of living a truly fulfilling life *while* on your journey of recovery.

Symptom resolution need not be a prerequisite for embarking on your recovery journey. Recovery can start for you right now as you begin reading this book.

How long your recovery takes, and what it takes to get there, will vary, as will what recovery means for each one of us, but the principles and mindsets to motivate and maintain this journey are largely shared.

WHO IS THIS BOOK FOR?

This workbook has been designed to help people at any stage of their journey.

- It can encourage those who are not in recovery to become aware of its possibility, believe in it and pursue it.
- It can encourage those already on their journey of recovery to stay on this path.
- It can also help those who have already *reached* a state of recovery to stay there.

This book focuses on helping you build a set of skills that can help you on the road to recovery from whatever your mental health issues may be. And while it contains insights and practices to help anticipate and prevent a crisis, it should never be used as a substitute for medical care, especially during a crisis.

MY JOURNEY TO RECOVERY

I'm proud to say that I am now living a life with serious mental illness in which I am *thriving*. But it was a long, hard road to this "recovery," filled with years of failed efforts, losses, disappointments, demoralization and stigma.

Before this, I was barely existing – merely surviving. I felt ashamed and embarrassed, hopeless and seemingly helpless. I had withdrawn and isolated myself from others, and even from myself. And so it remained for 14 years.

But then, quite suddenly in the depths of my despair, in the most unlikely of places – a psych ward – my hope for recovery was sparked. I was inspired by my peers. I saw examples of people who had faced mental health challenges like mine, yet had reached recovery and were now living *well*. And it gave me hope that I, too, could "get better." That flicker of hope allowed me to imagine the possibilities of a life in recovery.

FINDING MY WAY

I became determined to *reach* recovery, but the path I needed to take was unclear. There was no definitive guide. I didn't yet know where to access peer support, or even what peer support would look like in this context. My future still seemed so uncertain, so I was often confused, frustrated and afraid.

Although I had access to good medical treatment, I knew there was so much more that I had to figure out on my own. Although I had the loving support of my spouse, he seemed to lack hope in me at times, as he hadn't witnessed the examples of recovery in others that had so inspired *me*. I therefore often felt alone. It was incredibly challenging.

However, through seeking out more examples of peers living fulfilling lives with mental illness, I gradually discovered a whole community of us. I found out more about *their* experiences of illness and recovery, and I shared details of my own experiences. This helped inspire, support and guide me

5

on my own path to recovery – until, in 2018, I did it! I reached my own recovery point!

DEFINING WHAT RECOVERY MEANT FOR *ME*

Let's remind ourselves of something vital again here: recovery is not synonymous with being "cured." For me, it meant reaching a place where I was, and still am, able to pursue a safe, dignified and meaningful life that is not limited by my illness.

I made many mistakes and missteps on the way to this point, while also encountering much disappointment and heartache, but, with each challenge that I overcame, I grew stronger and wiser.

I'm pleased to say that I've been living in *my* version of recovery ever since 2018. While I pray to be in this place for the rest of my life, it is a never-ending journey – on which I work daily.

HELPING OTHERS WITH *THEIR* RECOVERY

As living a fulfilling life in recovery became a long-term reality for me, I realized that I wanted to make it my life's mission to inspire hope for recovery in *others* challenged by mental illness too.

So I now do this by sharing my lived experience – both the good and the bad. I do it in every way I can think of, with the aim of touching as many of my peers and their supporters as possible, especially those who may be struggling *most*, like psychiatric patients.

One of my initiatives to help by sharing lived experience was creating the ForLikeMinds peer support platform, which, at the time I'm writing this, includes a Facebook community of over 75,000 followers. I know the lessons I learned on my journey can be invaluable, so I feel deeply grateful that they've now reached so many people. Nearly every day people reach out to thank me for my help – for giving them hope. You see, we need each other, you and I. I need you. You need me. We help give each other's lives tremendous meaning and purpose.

We can all make important contributions to promoting recovery and helping people living with mental illness reach it. Because, although our supporters *support* us with our mental health, academics *study* us and clinicians *treat* us, it is only us who *live* through the experience of it. People living with mental illness are therefore experts by necessity – through their own experience. Ultimately, nobody can know us better than we do. That is why we can so profoundly impact each other. We must share our expertise directly and seize the opportunity to help each other learn from both our struggles and our successes. As when we empower each other in these ways, it greatly increases the chances of reaching and living in recovery.

My intention when writing this workbook was both to inform and empower as many people living with mental health struggles as I can. So it is my sincere hope that it can help and support you with *your* journey to recovery and living the wonderful, fulfilling life you deserve.

MAKING THIS WORK

Between us, you and I are going to make this work. Trust me. Let me be your recovery guide.

You are brave, courageous and much stronger than you think. After all, living with mental illness takes great stamina and resilience. And by reading this, you've taken a huge step already toward "getting better" and living your best life.

But I want to *help* you on your journey. Everyone needs a little help – there's no shame or weakness in that. On the contrary, it takes both great self-awareness and great strength to seek support. And I may know a few things about the journey ahead that you have not yet discovered.

For example, things may feel hard now. Maybe even *really* hard. Or seemingly impossible to deal with. You may be feeling sad, lonely or even hopeless. But let me assure you that today is not your forever. You will not always feel this way.

Recovery *is* a possibility – no matter how long you've been unwell. In fact, it may be closer than you think.

I hope in the course of this book to help you imagine what recovery might look like for *you* – and to reach it more easily. And I feel privileged to have the chance to do this.

However, it's also important to know from the outset that you won't reach a point of recovery by *just* reading this book, taking the advice of your healthcare providers and/or relying on the support of your loved ones. These things will all significantly *help*, of course, but, ultimately, recovery lies within *you* – in *your* outlook and *your* hopes for a better life. In the end, it's largely up to you to make it happen, and you *can*.

It's not easy to know what treatment and lifestyle changes will work for you. But with enough curiosity, exploration, hard work, discipline, commitment, resilience, patience and, of course, support from people like myself, your loved ones and/or health professionals, I have faith that you'll be able to figure out what works for you – and follow through with it.

ABOUT THE WORKBOOK

The goal of this workbook is to share insights and practices that empower you on your journey to live your best life.

It draws from a combination of:

- My own experience living with serious mental illness for over 20 years
- My observations of, and insights from, my peers
- The research into evidence-based treatment strategies that I have familiarized myself with, as part of my own recovery journey

As such, the pages that follow have been designed not only to offer *background insights* into a diverse range of concepts that I hope will help you on your journey, but also *practical strategies* that I hope will help you reach recovery.

THE POWER OF PEER SUPPORT

As already mentioned, many of the principles and practices in this workbook are inspired by, based on or reinforced by information and insights gained from peers, i.e., through "peer support."

The idea of peer support is based on the belief that people who have faced, endured and overcome adversity can offer useful encouragement, hope and perhaps even mentorship to others facing similar situations. It is an evidence-based approach that has been shown to improve mental health outcomes.

My hope is that this workbook is in itself a form of peer support, offering many of the same benefits as the kind of person-to-person peer support offered in other modalities and forums.

A 2014 analysis evaluating the efficacy of peer support by employed peer supporters in the treatment of serious mental illness revealed that it led to "reduced inpatient service use, improved relationships with healthcare providers, better engagement with care, higher levels of empowerment, increased patient activation, and also higher levels of hopefulness for recovery" (Chinman *et al.*, 2014). A narrative review conducted in 2017 found that being supported by employed peer supporters contributed to increases in "hope, empowerment and quality of life" (Bellamy *et al.*, 2017).

THEMES OF RECOVERY

This workbook covers a wide range of themes – 54 in total – all of which can be important on the road to recovery. These 54 themes are organized into eight broader chapters to help with ease of navigation, as explained further in "How to Use the Workbook" on page 15. The chapters are:

- **Self-assessment** – gives you the chance to raise your awareness of your mental health issues and take ownership of them
- **Life Plans** – reinforces the possibilities of living *well* with mental illness and encourages goal-setting
- **The Journey** – provides guidance on what to expect on the path to recovery and how to manage the recovery experience
- **Facing Challenges** – provides tools to help you deal with the inevitable challenges that you'll encounter on the road to recovery
- **Managing Emotions** – suggests effective strategies for managing and reframing emotional challenges
- **Treatment** – introduces and helps you explore individual treatment options across therapy, psychiatric care, medication, common health comorbidities, suicide prevention and crisis planning
- **Self-care** – discusses different self-care approaches, including alternative and complementary treatments
- **Relationships** – explores how to optimize support relationships to facilitate recovery

USE BY "SUPPORTERS" AND HEALTHCARE PROFESSIONALS

This workbook provides plenty of opportunities to involve the people I call your "supporters" on your path to recovery – whether they be loved ones, healthcare providers (psychiatrists, therapists and similar) and/or your peers. In fact, many of the suggestions in this workbook involve working with your supporters *directly* wherever possible.

I principally wrote this book for the people actually suffering from mental health challenges. My hope is that their "supporters" will *also* find it useful. If you're one of those "supporters," you might like to use it in any of the following ways:

- To increase your *own* understanding of strategies that you can facilitate and promote in the person, or people, you support
- To recommend as a purchase by, or give as a gift to, a person/people that you support to encourage them on the road to recovery
- To work through and complete *with* the person, or people, you support as part of their active involvement in the recovery journey

If you're a healthcare provider, for example, you might find it useful to acquire more insight into the recovery experience of your patients; you might choose to incorporate some elements of the peer-support based knowledge into your patient care in order to inspire and reinforce hope for recovery; or you might use the book to pursue engaging discussions on recovery, which can, in turn, enhance treatment outcomes through increased patient activation.

If you are a clinician, for example, you might recommend it either for home use or for in-office discussion in order to enhance continuity between visits – something that is facilitated by the deliberately concise style of the workbook and its exercises.

HOW TO USE THE WORKBOOK

Many workbooks are designed for the reader to work through and complete only in the order presented, with each section building upon earlier sections. You are welcome to take this approach here, too, if you like. However, all 54 sections in *this* workbook also largely stand alone, which means that they can, in theory, be completed in any order desired, depending on what themes you feel could be of most help to you at any given time.

At the same time, as already mentioned on page 12, the sections are grouped into eight wider categories, or chapters, that I hope will help you navigate the workbook more easily by identifying both the chapters *and* the sections that feel the most relevant to your circumstances.

I wanted to provide this flexibility of approach as recognition of the fact that each person's mental health recovery journey will be different, as it will be personal to *them*.

This means that some chapters may not feel as relevant to you as others do. I therefore suggest that you simply *start* with the chapters that you feel the most interested in learning more about and that you feel you can benefit *most* from and then progress from there.

We recommend that you keep a journal handy as you complete the exercises in this workbook. You can use the journal if you need more space to fully complete exercises and potentially take notes.

YOUR RECOVERY OATH

One section that I suggest every reader visits before turning to any other relevant sections, however, is the "Recovery Oath," which allows you to affirm, or reaffirm, your commitment to recovery.

Whether you are starting your recovery journey or fine-tuning specific aspects of it, this oath will serve to cement your goals in using this workbook.

By consciously recognizing these goals, you will be able to proceed with a much clearer sense of your mission and a deeper sense of commitment to getting the most out of this book.

THE STRUCTURE EXPLAINED

Both the Recovery Oath and, subsequently, each of the 54 themed sections in the book, are split into a "Goals" page and an "Exercise" page.

The Goals page discusses the theme in hand in general, offering a combination of background information, suggested focus points and related practical guidance, all of which I hope will help you reach recovery and stay there.

Each Goals page is followed by an accompanying Exercise page, which is designed to help you put the recovery-oriented strategies into *practice*. It is in these Exercise pages that you will find straightforward exercises based on self-reflection, learning and skill development. As such, the implementation of the Exercise pages is intended to *reinforce* the themes discussed in the Goals pages.

As you approach each section, try to keep an open mind. Give the new ideas and possibilities a chance. Not all of it may feel applicable to your particular situation, so focus on the topics you feel are most relevant to you. At the same time, try not to immediately dismiss the other goals as completely irrelevant to you. Instead, think about whether some of the goals might be applicable in ways you hadn't previously considered, or might be applicable at a later date, for example.

The workbook is also designed for you to be able to periodically revisit any Goals and Exercise pages that feel relevant as a part of their ongoing treatment. This will give you the chance to return to certain themes as and when you feel the need, allowing you to retry relevant exercises, reflect on how you're doing now versus before and potentially adapt any of the self-care strategies to your current situation, depending on where you are *now* in your recovery journey.

My hope is that this workbook will help you both work toward – and reach – recovery. And let's face it – you'll never know if you don't give it a shot. A little hope can open many possibilities. So be patient, be optimistic and who knows how well things might turn out …

On a practical note, you *might* want to choose a nice notebook of some sort to use in conjunction with this book – so that you can keep a note of your observations and discoveries all in one place along your road to recovery. If you ever choose to revisit certain themes and exercises, as suggested above, you should then easily be able to turn back and see how the exercise went the last time, versus now, if desired. You can also update your results and track your progress on specific exercises over time.

TROUBLESHOOTING ALONG THE WAY

It's completely normal to come up against a lot of challenges throughout the course of a recovery journey, so please do not allow yourself to be discouraged by them when they crop up. While this workbook is intended to help you *avoid* certain challenges, my hope is that it will also help you work *through* the ones that do appear on your path.

It's also important to remember that "relapse" is common. By relapse, I mean a recurrence of the symptoms arising from a mental illness, which may negatively impact your daily functioning.

The *primary* cause of relapse is medication non-adherence, so it's important to fully adhere to treatment and only explore adjustments over time in consultation with your doctor. However, *other* causes of relapse are often unavoidable.

You can, however, look out for the *signs* of relapse, as these usually begin with a change in how you're feeling and what you're doing – a deviation from your "normal" self.

If you notice any of these signs, it's important to seek help as soon as possible. It's also important to remember that a relapse does *not* mean a loss of the gains you've already made, or having to start all over again. If it happens, try to view it as nothing more than a bump in the road – one of the many potential challenges that you are going to persevere through, and "get over" – on your recovery journey.

You may not be able to *avoid* a relapse, but you can't let it stop you from pursuing recovery. You can't let it make you give up!

After all, every challenge that we overcome helps to build up our bank of *experience* on the road to recovery, which means that, in the future, such challenges are likely to feel less worrying and more manageable.

This workbook is intended to help you manage such challenges, or "bumps" along the way – and, in so doing, help your road to recovery feel less daunting and more achievable. If you get lost or distracted on this journey, it's my hope that this workbook will help guide you back onto the right road.

YOUR RECOVERY OATH

Recovery is a journey to reach the life you want to live and become a better and truer *you*. Many people with mental illness don't believe this is possible. They've never seen examples, or people have given them the impression that they'll always be sick. However, recovery *is* possible – through your own hope, efforts, energies and commitment! Don't wait a minute longer to begin your journey.

Although your recovery will not necessarily be symptom free, your symptoms can be minimized so they do not hold you back. With the right approach, sometimes you may even feel symptom-free.

The journey to recovery likely won't be straightforward. The path can be rough and tumble. Setbacks are common, and sometimes you may feel stuck. However, if you focus on your strengths, you can overcome these challenges and continue moving forward.

Patience and resilience are critical, as slow and steady often wins the race. Trying something different can often be useful, too. Rest when you need to along the path, but never quit and never be afraid to ask for a little help. Having the love and support of your friends and family, as well as the best medical treatment possible, is critical. A "team" approach often works best. Now, get on your way. The whole you, the true you, is waiting for you.

Take this recovery oath, to accept and affirm the principles that will guide you in your recovery journey. Modify it however you wish. Make it yours.

I, [_____],
do solemnly swear that each and every day I will:

1. Know that I deserve recovery

2. Disempower self-stigma

3. Never lose hope

4. Pursue and live the life I want

5. Take responsibility for myself

6. Work hard to reach recovery

7. Ask for, and accept, help and support

8. Seek the best treatment possible

9. Adhere to my treatment

10. Try my best to cope with challenges

11. Practice lots of self-care

12. Continue on my journey of recovery no matter what

SELF-ASSESSMENT

1

LOVING YOURSELF

GOALS

Loving yourself is a beautiful thing. Always know that you are special even if you are struggling. Be kind, gentle and forgiving to yourself. You are loved and mean a lot to many people, even though it may not always feel like it.

Mental illness can make you think: "Who could *possibly* love *me*?" As a result, you may feel unloved, unlovable, or you may even hate yourself at times. You may ruminate on these thoughts, but this kind of stigmatized thinking cannot be trusted, and you must not listen to it. Sometimes you may be the person who is hardest on yourself, but you don't deserve to be treated so harshly; it only makes things worse.

Sometimes others may also make you feel like you're unloved, they're tired of you and your illness, and they can't put up with you anymore. Remember that they are reacting to the illness, not you! Try not to push away the people who care about you out of fear that they'll eventually abandon you. Having said that, not everyone is in your corner. Be sure to focus on the people who count in your life and not that insensitive friend or family member who may have turned their back on you.

The truth is that you're a wonderful person. You have so many amazing qualities, some of which may be unknown to you. Mental illness may be blinding you to these, even though your friends and family can see them. You probably aren't giving yourself enough credit, if any at all. Remember, self-love is critical to recovery. You have to love *you* first and foremost, before turning your attention to others. Loving yourself makes you realize you are worthy of a better life. When you love yourself, you're much more likely to believe you deserve recovery.

EXERCISE

Indicate which of the following statements describe you. Then, ask a loved one to indicate which statements describe you. Afterward, compare the two lists. Accept their praise.

Repeat these affirmations daily. You can also write them down on a card you can refer to. Work every day to realize more of these qualities. And remember, unconditional love is important too.

I am loved.	I am honest.
I am needed.	I am hopeful.
I am worthy.	I am inspiring.
I am good enough.	I am kind to others.
I am affectionate.	I am kind to myself.
I am amazing.	I am lovable.
I am compassionate.	I am loving.
I deserve good things.	I prioritize me.
I love myself.	I take care of myself.
I am empathetic.	I enjoy my solitude.
I am funny.	My needs and wants are valid.
I am generous.	My feelings are valid.
I am gentle.	I am selfless.
I am helpful.	I am smart.

2

FINDING HOPE

GOALS

Hope is wishing for something good and believing that it is possible. Hope is not *waiting* for this good to happen, but being active in *making* it happen. This is critical to reaching recovery.

The power of hope cannot be overestimated. You must always try to maintain hope despite the many challenges you may have faced and continue to face, whether they be years of failed efforts, repeated losses, discrimination or demoralization.

Remember that you've overcome difficulties in the past, so you can do it again, and find hope in that. Never give up on that hope, as it can inspire you, motivate you and keep you going through the darkest of times. However, as hard as you may try to hold on to this hope, you may well feel like you've lost sight of it at times. Please know that this is normal – for everyone. Remember that hope is often dormant, waiting to be awoken. This means that it is *always* there, even when you can't *feel* it in the present moment. As such, it can return at any time – sometimes when you least expect it.

Also, remember that the hope you need doesn't exist within you alone. It can come from all sorts of other sources, such as friends, family, caregivers, peers (especially other peers in recovery), animals or faith. Having others accept, love, support, value and believe in you can be a powerful source of hope. Importantly, your healthcare providers can bolster your hope by giving you encouraging feedback and communicating their confidence in your ability to recover. They can talk to you about a future not limited by your illness. Believing you deserve better and acting like you do sustains the hope that can fuel your recovery journey. Embrace hope. Let it drive you and let it be with you. Never lose hope for hope.

EXERCISE

Hope can be hard to figure out and embrace in your life, especially because it combines past, present and future. Hope is often achieved by finding strength and motivation in our past experiences in order to address the challenges which are currently standing in the way of our goals. It's therefore useful to ask yourself some critical questions about hope and reflect on them thoughtfully.

- How do you define hope?

- Do you feel like you have hope?

- What makes you hopeful?

- Who makes you feel hopeful?

- What has made you hopeful in the past?

- Was there a time in the past you lost hope? If so, how did you regain it?

- Is anything keeping you from being hopeful at the moment? If so, how can you get past this?

- How can you increase your sense of hope moving forward?

3

MEASURING AND NURTURING HOPE

GOALS

Hope is good. Hope captures the power and resilience of the human spirit. It can come from many sources – from within, from the love and support of friends and family, from peer support and from a supportive community.

You may feel like your family and friends don't always have hope for you, but they probably do.

You can also find hope in peers who are fighting to reach or have reached recovery.

Your treatment provider should have hope for you too. If you feel they don't, talk to them about it or consider getting a new one.

Hope can and will deliver us from mental illness to a full and meaningful life. It can make what felt impossible possible, and can help you reach recovery.

EXERCISE

It can be useful to regularly assess how hopeful you feel in life so that you know where you stand on this front and can decide how to nurture *more* hope in your life.

How hopeful are you? To the following affirmations, respond: 1 – yes, 2 - sometimes, 3 – no.

Celebrate the 1s, work on the 2s and really work on the 3s, considering from which sources you can draw more hope in each case.

I deserve a better life.

I can be happy again.

I believe in recovery.

I know I can reach recovery.

I know I will reach recovery.

I am trying to have hope.

I should have hope.

I am acting on my hope now.

I have short-term goals.

I have long-term goals.

I am loved and needed.

I have support to reach recovery.

I am not ashamed or embarrassed.

I reject stigma.

I reject self-stigma.

I am strong and resilient.

I am optimistic.

I can overcome challenges.

I know my treatment will work.

I am doing the best I can to get better.

I have faith that things will work out.

4

RECOGNIZING STIGMA

GOALS

Conversations around mental health are often mired in deeply harmful stigma. The most common and harmful type of external stigma is "public stigma," or the negative or discriminatory views society holds toward people with mental illness. Some may say we're scary, weak, lazy, stupid, unable to contribute to society, attention-seeking and/or unpredictable. They may even say we're violent. All of this can be extremely hurtful, and it influences how people and institutions treat us.

It can be difficult to ignore these biases. You may face discrimination in treatment by healthcare providers, employment, housing and the criminal justice system, among other areas. Stigma may lead someone with mental illness to delay or avoid seeking treatment (Corrigan, 2004), which may worsen your condition and ultimate outcomes. However, it is important to realize that discrimination exists toward our community as it does toward other minorities. You need to know when you're being discriminated against and how to address it.

There are, of course, legal ways to address discrimination at the local, state and federal levels. We have to carefully consider protesting unjust treatment by institutions that discriminate against us.

It's different when stigma comes from individuals, and they may not have the same impact on our day-to-day lives. We may become highly sensitive to it. But we must know that it is based on ignorance. For example, while some believe people with mental illness are violent, in truth they are more likely to be victims of crime than perpetrators.

Fundamentally, stigma is based on lies. Some people will unintentionally stigmatize you, but it can still be hurtful. If the stigmatizing actions of people you care about are hurting you, speak up and let them know. Ask them to clarify their stigmatizing statements and try to educate them. You can tell them what sorts of statements you find hurtful and ask them not to say them. If they're understanding, they will respect you and your concerns. You have to give them this chance, as you don't want to break off relationships with people who care for you. You can't let stigma do that to you.

EXERCISE

Explore your own experience of, and relationship with, social stigma by asking yourself the questions below, maybe even writing your answers somewhere so that you can come back to them and reassess them at a later point.

- What are the most common types of stigma you experience?

- Are there people you care about who make stigmatizing statements or act in stigmatizing ways toward you, whether you feel they are intentional or not?

- How do their statements or actions make you feel? How could people change their words or actions to help you?

You may now want to gently share your observations with your loved ones, in particular anyone you've identified as stigmatizing you in some way, so that they have the chance to address any inappropriate or hurtful behavior, improve their relationship with you and help you on your journey to recovery.

5

RECOGNIZING *SELF*-STIGMA

GOALS

The impact of stigma is amplified when we internalize it. It's when we start believing stigma to be true that it becomes self-stigma. There are five categories of self-stigma defined by Ritsher (Ritsher *et al.*, 2003):

1. **Alienation** – feeling out of place, inferior, disappointing or misunderstood
2. **Stereotype endorsement** – accepting harmful stereotypes, for example, that people with mental illness are violent, shouldn't get married, can't make decisions, can't contribute to society or can't live a good life
3. **Discrimination** – believing you are being discriminated against, patronized, ignored or not taken seriously even when there's no apparent reason to think so
4. **Social withdrawal** – feeling a need to self-protect by self-isolating, likely to involve avoiding getting close to others, socializing or talking about yourself
5. **Anticipated stigma** – an *expectation* that you'll be stigmatized

The emotional impact of self-stigma is often greater than the symptoms of mental illness itself. It batters our self-esteem, self-efficacy and outlook on life, sometimes making us lose hope that we can ever get better. The shame and embarrassment can make us reluctant to seek help and talk about our condition. It can also cause us to engage in self-sabotaging behavior because we expect failure.

Rumination on negative thoughts about self-stigma is common. We may generalize our experiences of stigma. If we've experienced stigma a few times, we may assume that others who do not stigmatize us will also have stigmatizing views about us. This is known as perceived stigma, and can limit understanding and awareness, allowing our self-stigma to grow even stronger. Self-stigma may even cause you to disassociate yourself from other people living with mental illness, which may reduce your potential support network.

If left unaddressed, this vicious cycle can lead to worse outcomes, especially if you're already struggling in other ways. Therefore, understanding and addressing self-stigma is an essential part of healing and recovering from mental illness. You need to know that stigma lies, and that stigma is not your problem, but the problem of those who stigmatize you. You can overcome stigma and self-stigma through self-empowerment.

EXERCISE

Answering the following questions may help you identify if you suffer from self-stigma:

- Do you believe any stereotypes about your mental illness to be true? If so, which ones?

- Are you embarrassed about your mental illness?

- Do you feel less capable than before your diagnosis?

- If you're isolating from others or avoiding contact with people, what are the reasons?

The following questions may help you combat self-stigma:

- Do people without mental illness ever exhibit some of the stereotypes associated with mental illness?

- Can you do anything to change or control the behaviors you associate with your mental illness?

- What challenges have you faced in the past and what skills have helped you overcome them?

6

VALUING SOCIAL ROLES

GOALS

Mental illness is a part of you, but not *all* of you. Make sure to remind people of this if you hear them suggest otherwise, even if it's unintentional. They should remember, as should you, that, in many ways, living with a serious mental illness is no different from living with a serious physical illness – you should never let it define you.

After all, you have many valuable roles in life, and they all contribute to who you are as a friend, partner, family member, student, work colleague, community member; the list goes on. You may well feel like you lost some, or even all, of these roles when you became ill. If so, you're likely to crave being your "normal" pre-illness self again. It's therefore important to recognize that you still are that same person at your core. You hold the same value as you did before your illness, if not more, given that living with an illness can often allow you to understand the struggles of other people better.

You may have "withdrawn" from some of your old roles in life when you became unwell out of fear that these communities would no longer accept you because you don't feel like yourself. You may feel like you're an imposter now, that you're no longer "successful" or that you're no longer a good friend because you have a mental illness, but you're wrong. It's likely that many people miss you – many more than you might think. As such, it is important to give people the benefit of the doubt. Most will accept you just as you are, rather than expecting you to be what you feel you "should" be.

Sometimes it takes a community to overcome mental illness. Don't be afraid to be a part of this. Although it's not all of you, be proud to have a mental illness. Living with it day by day is an accomplishment. Be proud of *all* of you.

EXERCISE

We all have a wide range of roles that we "play" in life and that help make up who we consider ourselves to be – whether that is a friend, sibling, parent, child, worker, colleague, hobbyist, home maintainer, student, teacher, volunteer, caregiver, pet owner, religious practitioner, member of a minority group such as racial, ethnic or LGBTQ+ communities, or whatever else.

It's important to be aware of how vital these social roles are to us and to know that we don't have to give up these roles just because we suffer from mental illness.

- What do you consider your most important roles in life?

- What can you do to be more active in these roles while you're on the road to your mental health recovery?

- What additional social roles would you like to pursue?

7

NURTURING YOUR SENSE OF SELF

GOALS

There is strong evidence that developing or rediscovering a sense of self can significantly improve the chance of recovery for people with mental illness. To achieve, or increase, this sense of self in the face of mental illness, it is vital to recognize that your mental illness does not define you, to appreciate the possibilities in life outside of your mental illness and to take an active role in your treatment planning.

The recovery process can be viewed through four key "sense of self" stages, as described below:

1. **Discovering a More Active Self** – realizing the possibility that you can act in your own interest
2. **Taking Stock of the Self** – starting to recognize your new or rediscovered sense of self and the possibilities for change that this brings, as a result of acting in your own interest
3. **Putting the Self into Action** – building on your growing confidence in your sense of self through personal action
4. **Appealing to the Self** – accessing an enhanced sense of self as a source of refuge from mental illness, which can be deeply empowering (Davidson et al., 1992)

These stages are largely about accepting your own mental illness and taking more control of its treatment. This can involve, for example, coordinating the work of your treatment team – such as your doctor, therapist and other supporters – so that the support you receive is invited and welcome, rather than in any way imposed. The sense of self that this kind of control helps to develop can contribute to increased receptivity and supporter engagement on your part. This is, in turn, likely to improve both your support relationships and your recovery outcomes.

EXERCISE

Look at the four "sense of self" stages described on page 39 and use the prompts below to help figure out how you might be able to nurture and grow your own sense of self moving forward.

- Which of the four "sense of self" stages do you feel you are at?

- What actions could you take to move to the next stage?

- By now, you should know that your mental illness does not define you. Take a little time to think about what you feel *does* define you.

LIFE PLANS

8

KNOWING YOUR MEANING AND PURPOSE IN LIFE

GOALS

A sense of meaning and purpose in life is critical to being happy and healthy. Most people know what *doesn't* make them happy, such as an unfulfilling career or bad relationships. Such things may even *contribute* to mental illness. However, people tend to find it harder to know what *does* make them happy, or happier. We can often be strongly influenced by what other people – like our friends, family, community or wider society – think should make us happy. But their views may well be influenced by stigma and other biases, so it's important to figure out what gives your life meaning for yourself.

You can start this by determining your core values, identified by the VIA Institute (VIA Institute, n.d.), which is "dedicated to the science of character strengths." They outline core values as:

1. **Wisdom** – including creativity, curiosity, judgement, love of learning and perspective
2. **Courage** – including bravery, honesty, perseverance and zest
3. **Humanity** – including kindness, love and social intelligence
4. **Justice** – including fairness, leadership and teamwork
5. **Temperance** – including forgiveness, humility, prudence and self-regulation
6. **Transcendence** – including an appreciation of beauty and excellence, gratitude, hope, humor and spirituality

Taking the time to assess the importance of each of these in your own life can help you define your sense of meaning and purpose. It's important in this process of self-reflection and self-discovery to try to find a good balance between the values that mean the most to you by identifying and implementing regular activities that will help you fulfill them.

It can be hard to be happy if you feel that you're living someone else's life. It can sap you of your motivation to get better. On the other hand, you're much more likely to be energized and motivated when you're doing the things that *you* think are best. Don't feel guilty about disappointing others. This is *your* life. Knowing your meaning and purpose in it can help you to fully embrace the possibilities of living a life in recovery.

EXERCISE

Renowned German psychologist Erich Fromm once defined meaning and purpose in life as "caring for someone or something, being active and creative in developing one's life, being part of a home or community, identifying oneself as a separate individual from others and living an authentic life, and having order in life" (Fromm, 1956).

Take some time to come up with, and write down, your *own* definition of meaning and purpose – along the lines of the above but with activities and ways of being that particularly resonate with *you* as having great value in life. Asking yourself the following questions may help you with this.

- What are your key values?

- What would you say your sense of meaning and purpose in life was *before* you got sick? Even if you had never taken the time to *specifically* define such things, think about what consistently made you feel most content and fulfilled. It's important not to lose sight of these things.

- What qualities, activities, ways of being, people, places or anything else make you feel most contented and fulfilled *now*? How could you incorporate these more into your daily life?

9

ESTABLISHING LIFE GOALS

GOALS

Life goals allow you to put your meaning and purpose into *action*, and are critical to reaching recovery. Think about what would make you leap out of bed every day to work toward, and you'll be well on your way to identifying some authentic life goals for yourself. It may feel difficult to imagine such positivity and motivation right now, but please don't worry about this, as it's in no way unusual when you're sick to find things like this hard.

For most people with mental illness, life goals include staying well through medical treatment, self-care, meaningful work and healthy relationships. Make sure you get the best professional treatment and take good care of yourself. Make sure you pursue a career that you feel will make you happy, and don't feel bad if you decide to do something your loved ones, or wider society, don't seem to approve of. Be sure to seek out genuine, trusting relationships – people with mental illness need deeper connections than we might experience in casual relationships. And yes, you *can* have such genuine connections, even *with* your mental health issues. You *can* have significant others and children if you want. It's only *you* who determines your life goals. This is self-determination, and it is key to reaching recovery.

Do not accept the low expectations of others. They may caution you against pursuing certain goals out of fear you won't be able to handle the stress. Recognize the risks of doing nothing. Also recognize the potential risks of *pursuing* your goals upfront, and plan around these. For example, if you feel that becoming overwhelmed is a risk, aim to achieve one goal before moving on to the next. Make your goals adaptable to changing circumstances. Consider the factors that could help you as well as those holding you back from achieving your goals. Don't let your mental illness hold you back.

It's not too late to pursue your goals, and it's never too late to live your dreams. Knowing, and feeling excited by, your life goals is the greatest motivation you'll ever have to get well, so it's worth spending time establishing and embracing them. Sometimes the greatest obstacle you'll ever face is how you feel about yourself.

EXERCISE

Now that you know what a significant role working toward positive life goals can play in helping you achieve a happier, healthier life, you'll understand just how important it is to spend time *establishing* your own life goals and how to start "living" these. The questions below will hopefully help you with this:

- What would you say your top three life goals were before you got sick? Even if you had never taken the time to specifically define such goals, think about what was most important to you and what you found yourself generally drawn to and moving toward?

- What are your top three life goals now? Really think into these, and then visualize yourself achieving and living your goals.

- For each of your three current goals, identify:

  1. What's the first step, or next step, that I can take toward this?

  2. What are the potential risks and how can I prepare for these?

  3. Who can help me move toward these goals?

10

BACK TO SCHOOL

GOALS

High school and college students with mental illness often experience difficulties completing their studies. But even if you do have to drop out or take medical leave, it's always possible to return. You're never too old to pursue and achieve your academic goals, even if you've fallen a bit behind your friends. There's nothing to be embarrassed about.

Having a mental illness might make it difficult to cope with school stressors, such as academic pressure, career uncertainty, financial concerns and relationship issues. These things might even trigger or worsen conditions such as anxiety or depression. Many students are afraid to ask for help and consequently experience loneliness, isolation and a lack of critical support.

However, high schools and colleges often offer a range of helpful resources these days that can help students address their stressors. For example, a college counseling office can refer students for emotional support, and campus clubs and organizations can help address loneliness. A disabilities office may be able to offer reasonable accommodations under the *American with Disabilities Act* (*Americans with Disabilities Act, 1990*, n.d.) and *Rehabilitation Act* (*Rehabilitation Act, 1973*, n.d.), like giving more time to complete assignments and advice on whether medical leave could be a good option for you. While taking medical leave instead of dropping out may make it easier to return to school once you're well, there are still many issues to consider, such as the status of coursework, tuition payments and loans, so it's important to get guidance on this.

A financial aid office may also be able to provide financial assistance if needed. Supported education programs found through organizations such as Clubhouse International can also help.

Free adult education programs can help you develop basic skills or complete key qualifications, such as your GED. You can also check what services are available through your state's vocational rehabilitation office. A degree can also enhance your career opportunities and earnings potential. Don't give up on the education goals you had before becoming unwell. Many people living with mental illness have college degrees and you can too.

EXERCISE

It's important not to let your mental health issues trick you into thinking that you're not capable or worthy of academic or other learning achievements. As such, it's invaluable to dedicate a little time to exploring what you would really like on this front.

- What were your education goals before you got sick, and what are they now?

- How can achieving your current education goals help you pursue your current life goals?

- If you dropped out or took medical leave because of your illness, would you like to return to school?

- If you're still at school or college, are you making full use of the resources available to help address the challenges of your mental illness? Is there someone in the school staff or administration who can help you to access these resources?

11

FINDING EMPLOYMENT

GOALS

Meaningful work is often a top recovery goal for people with mental illness, and can be one of the most important factors for sustained recovery. As such, it's important to know from the outset that people with mental illness *can* make important contributions to the workforce. More often than not, they are ambitious, motivated, intelligent and able to handle stress. Contrary to what stigma might say, most are not "too sick" to work.

The biggest challenges for people with mental illness to pursue their chosen careers are often stigma and self-doubt. There are many contributing factors to this negative thinking, including high unemployment rates for people with mental illness, high rates of dropping out of college due to illness, a reluctance among people who *have* dropped out to return to school, a general lack of confidence and a presumption that work is simply no longer a possibility. However, despite these challenges, many people living with mental illness are successfully employed. It's usually a case of considering *different* career options, ensuring you can prioritize your mental health and developing coping strategies to manage workplace stresses.

An important initial step is to carefully consider your career interests. *What Color is Your Parachute?* by Richard Nelson Bolles (Bolles *et al.*, 1970) is a great book to help with this. Your state's vocational rehabilitation office may also be able to assist you. You might even want to consider a career as a Certified Peer Specialist where you can put your lived experience of mental health issues to use.

There are also laws and programs that may be able to help people with mental illness secure and maintain suitable employment. Employers may be required under the *Americans with Disabilities Act (Americans with Disabilities Act*, 1990, n.d.) to offer "reasonable accommodations" to people living with disabilities to make it easier for them to do their work. Examples include time off for doctor's appointments or a quiet workspace. Once you *do* have a job, it's best to have an open relationship with your manager, so you can get help early if you need it.

Having a valued working life is important for everyone, so never give up on your dreams of having meaningful work, because it *is* possible.

EXERCISE

What are your current work goals? What steps can you take now to pursue those goals?

If you would like to seek employment, here are a few avenues to consider:

1. Ask for help from friends and supporters. Maybe even seek out a mentor.
2. Volunteering can be a great way to develop skills, build confidence and obtain references that will help you when you apply for jobs. Volunteering with organizations that help underserved or at-risk communities might also help you to find your sense of meaning and purpose.
3. Explore the option of becoming a Certified Peer Specialist to help other people with mental illness to pursue recovery.
4. Seeking employment may be facilitated by Supported Employment-IPS and Assertive Community Treatment programs. Check offerings at Clubhouses.
5. Get to know your rights as a person with mental health issues in the workplace. For example, as already mentioned, the *Americans with Disabilities Act* may require employers to provide people with mental illness "reasonable accommodations" that can make it easier for them to do their job.

12

BENEFITING FROM EVIDENCE-BASED PRACTICES

GOALS

Evidence-based programs (EBPs) are proven by scientific studies to be effective. There are EBPs specifically designed to help people living with mental illness to achieve their goals. Key examples include supported education, supported employment and permanent supportive housing (SAMHSA, n.d.).

Supported education helps people with mental illness pursue education and training to return to school. It is individualized and prioritizes your preferences, strengths and experiences.

Supported employment helps people with mental illness find and keep meaningful jobs in the community. One approach is IPS, which helps you to choose, secure and keep competitive employment while receiving ongoing individualized long-term support.

Permanent supportive housing helps people with mental illness secure and keep housing that is decent, safe, affordable and integrated into the community.

All these programs focus on personal choice and recovery. Clubhouses or community behavioral health centers can usually help you access these programs. However, they can be hard to find, and many more are needed.

Two additional helpful EBPs are Integrated Treatment for Co-occurring Disorders (ITCD) (SAMHSA, n.d.) and Family Psychoeducation (FPE) (SAMHSA, n.d.). In ITCD, people with mental illness are able to receive treatment for substance use disorders at the same time as mental health issues. In FPE, you are given help to work better with your family. It offers people with mental illness and their families valuable information, helps them build social supports and enhances problem-solving, communication and coping skills. It is similar to family therapy in some respects, which many people find helpful.

In short, there are lots of programs out there that can help you and your supporters. So make sure you do your research, and seek as much help with this as you can. Don't say nothing works if you haven't tried all the options.

EXERCISE

- What additional supports do you think would be helpful for you to have to pursue your goals?

- Can a loved one, supporter or treatment provider help you get access to available evidence-based programs?

- What's stopping you from accessing programs available to help you reach and stay in recovery?

Clubhouses can help. A Clubhouse such as Fountain House is a place that offers people living with mental illness social support and help with their living needs and problems. You'll find a directory of Clubhouses at Clubhouse International. The FindTreatment.gov website can also help, providing a confidential and anonymous resource for persons seeking treatment for mental and substance use disorders (SAMHSA, n.d.).

13

MANAGING FINANCIAL MATTERS

GOALS

It's not uncommon for people with mental illness to have financial challenges from time to time. Don't be ashamed of your financial situation. This can adversely impact your mental health and is one of the greatest barriers to financial wellness. Many people experience financial hardship, and it can be addressed. Sometimes people will be unable to work due to their illness, or they may be reluctant to work because they fear they might lose their benefits. Yet having enough money to pay for the basic necessities of life as well as things that make life a bit more enjoyable is important for good mental health.

Some people may be able to rely on savings, family assistance or loans. Others are fortunate to have an income through part-time or full-time work. If you were employed before your became sick, be sure to check if you have insurance coverage for short-term or long-term disability. When you're well and able to work, it's financially prudent to save some of your income in case you are unable to work at times in the future. This will remove some of the fear and uncertainty about what will happen if you get sick and are once again unable to work.

As you plan and work toward personal financial health and wellbeing, consider the following objectives. There are many public and private resources available to help you pursue these goals, including non-profit and community groups, government agencies, social workers and personal finance professionals.

- **Financial security** – seek to earn income and manage spending to live a fulfilling lifestyle within your means. Build savings and assets that can help pay for future expected and unplanned needs.

- **Financial self-reliance** – seek to manage and allocate financial resources according to personal goals and values. Be able to support yourself without over reliance on others to achieve these goals and values.
- **Financial engagement** – seek to contribute to causes and your community to enhance your sense of value and help others.

Consider the resources you currently have and obstacles to achieve these goals.

Until you have enough resources to support your needs, you may consider government benefits, whether on a short-term or long-term basis. However, many people are unaware of what benefits they may be entitled to, and the enrollment processes can be complicated, so it's important to educate yourself about this.

The most important US government benefits are Supplemental Security Income (SSI), Social Security Disability Insurance (SSDI), Medicaid and Medicare, Veteran Affairs' benefits, food stamps and public housing programs. There are government benefit programs that allow you to earn up to a certain amount (usually through part-time work) and may allow you to continue to collect full medical benefits. Be sure to check your health insurance, if you have coverage, for short-term and long-term disability. Just bear in mind that, if you apply for this, you will need medical evidentiary support for your request and must be careful when completing your applications. Places such as community behavioral health centers may be able to help you with the application process. Certain non-profits can also offer assistance.

Get to know the resources available in your community, and consider these benefits if you need help. Don't feel bad about claiming these benefits if you need to – it is very hard to get and stay well without adequate financial resources and you shouldn't feel guilty about accepting any help to which you're entitled.

EXERCISE

Keeping a budget is important to maintaining financial health. According to the "Balanced Money Formula" (Warren *et al.*, 2005) based on after-tax income, you should aim to spend less than 50% on needs, about 30% on wants and save 20%.

Needs include housing, utilities, healthcare, transportation, insurance, basic groceries and basic clothing.

Wants are everything else: cable TV, cell phones, haircuts, swimming lessons, dog food, charity, books, vacations, etc.

Savings includes retirement accounts, emergency savings and debt repayment.

It's always good to prioritize spending according to first needs and then preferences. It's essential to prioritize and plan for scheduled payments on things like loans, housing, utilities and other critical recurring expenses.

Strategies to reduce other spending include medication discount programs, discounts available for people with disabilities, payment plans, such as payment deferments and debt consolidation programs.

It's okay to dip into any savings you have from time to time, but try to limit this. We all need to save for rainy days, and knowing that you have those extra "just-in-case funds" is likely to be a big comfort to you and help your overall mental health.

- List three wants and three needs below.

Wants:
1.
2.
3.

Needs:
1.
2.
3.

14

GETTING TO KNOW YOUR NEIGHBORHOOD

GOALS

Where you live matters to your mental health. There are many characteristics of a neighborhood that may be conducive to good mental health, though they will obviously be balanced against financial and other considerations.

You can learn a lot about a neighborhood just by walking around and talking to local residents. Desirable communities for you and your family will offer accessible and affordable medical care, desirable schools, meaningful employment opportunities, quality housing and childcare, and, ideally, also have good amenities, such as farmers markets.

Options for socialization and community integration are also important. It's great to spend time with peers, but you need to meet and spend time with *other* people too. They can help you realize just how multidimensional you are. If it's possible to be close to family or other loved ones, it can make it easier to access emotional support when needed. Public services, including libraries, houses of worship and community centers, can also help combat loneliness and offer self-care opportunities, as can Clubhouses if there are any in your area.

Amenities like green spaces and good areas for walks can encourage you to exercise. Availability of healthy food at retailers and farmers markets can help improve your diet. Good public transportation, including reasonable proximity to work, will allow you to get around more easily. Moreover, low crime rates may enhance safety and reduce stress levels by giving you a sense of security.

All of these are referred to as "social determinants" of mental health. They can all impact your mental health and physical health, which is why it is important to take them into consideration. You cannot separate who you are from where you live, so take a look around you. Are you living in the best neighborhood for you? If not, you might want to think about moving if your budget allows it. And if you *are* considering a move, be sure to carefully research your options based on all of the factors above.

EXERCISE

Take a walk and explore your neighborhood. Make a list of:

- The activities and places that can help you manage your mental health

- The activities and places of interest to you that you'd like to learn more about

Then, make a plan to visit these places.

If your budget allows it, consider taking positive mental health getaways, whether via public transportation, bike or car. Where could you easily get to *near* your neighborhood that would help enhance your mental health and keep you on the road to recovery?

THE JOURNEY

15

BEFORE YOUR JOURNEY

GOALS

Mental illness can go undetected and undiagnosed for a long time, as many people don't know the signs to watch for at the time of onset. A significant percentage of people go without treatment due to stigma, ignorance and misinformation. It can often take as long as ten years from symptom onset to treatment. If it's taken you this long, don't feel bad. You're not alone.

Onset of mental health issues can be gradual or sudden. Many people may attribute symptoms to current stressors, which they think are normal and will pass. Many will only seek help when their symptoms begin to interfere with life activities, and others may experience a full-blown episode, which may in some cases require hospitalization.

A diagnosis may be emotionally distressing. As a result, many deny their diagnoses and are hopeful that things will pass. Such people may refuse any treatment, which can make a condition worse and harder to treat. Common reactions to a diagnosis include shock, confusion, self-stigma, denial, despair, hopelessness, depression, grief and anger. You may have refused to accept treatment, experienced years of nonadherence or suffered multiple relapses. However, now is the time to accept treatment and do what is best for you.

Many people are fearful that they will no longer be able to pursue their life goals and may grieve their "lost" self – the person they and their loved ones thought they might be before they became ill. They and you may no longer think optimistically about the future. If this is the case, you may have been conditioned to always expect the worst.

For all of these reasons, paralyzingly low self-esteem, self-worth and demoralization are common. Even after you've started treatment, these feelings may last for years and significantly delay the start of your recovery journey. But it's vital to know that recovery is possible no matter how long you've been unwell. The initial steps of the recovery journey are nearly always the hardest.

EXERCISE

- What was receiving a diagnosis like for you?

- Do you accept your diagnosis?

- What actions have you taken to address your diagnosis?

- Are you receiving treatment?

- What parts of your life has your diagnosis and treatment changed, if any?

16

ALL ABOUT SELF

GOALS

Recovery is not something you take like a pill or that someone does for you. It's all about the self! You must take responsibility for managing your illness. Only you can do the hard work needed. You may be lacking in motivation at times, but you will need to find it and pull it from within.

Discipline can help when you're lacking motivation. There will be times when you feel like giving up, and you may temporarily do so. However, if you're going to reach recovery, you have to get your "self" back into the game. The hope that kick-starts your journey can amplify the potential of the self. It can boost self-esteem, self-determination and self-advocacy, all of which are essential to reaching recovery.

Self-esteem is how you feel about yourself, in both positive and negative terms. This can often be demonstrated through your actions. Do you treat yourself as well as you treat your friends in both good and bad times? If not, you may be lacking in self-esteem and need to learn to see yourself through a more positive lens, recognizing that you deserve better in life.

Self-determination is having the desire to do what you want with your life and doing what it takes to achieve it. Others may provide valuable guidance and support, but making the key decisions in your life is down to you. You know your wants and needs better than anyone else, and pursuing these goals can be the greatest motivator to get well.

Self-advocacy is speaking up for yourself by making sure people know your wants and needs, and letting them know when they don't respect these. This can be intimidating, and you may risk losing friends when you stand up to them about their behavior. It takes real courage to speak up, but you have it in you. It's hard to respect ourselves when others are disrespecting us.

EXERCISE

Here are a few statements in the Rosenberg Self-esteem Scale (Rosenberg, 1965) to help you reflect on your self-esteem. Do you agree or disagree with each of these? It may be helpful to talk to a therapist about your answers.

- I feel that I am a person of worth, at least on an equal plane with others.

- I feel that I have many good qualities.

- All in all, I am inclined to feel that I am a failure.

- I can do things as well as most other people.

- I feel I do not have much to be proud of.

- I take a positive attitude toward myself.

- Overall, I am satisfied with myself.

- I wish I could have more respect for myself.

- I certainly feel useless at times.

- At times I think I am no good at all.

17

STARTING YOUR JOURNEY

GOALS

The recovery journey often begins with accepting that you have an illness and you need help. Although stigma and fear may stand in your way, it is better to accept help sooner rather than later. Accepting your illness and overcoming the fear of it is critical. Another big step is accepting medical treatment and in many cases recognizing that you may have to take medication – possibly for the rest of your life.

We all wish that our mental illness would just go away, but it likely won't. This is something you have to come to terms with. The recovery journey is not about running from your illness but running *with* it. The start of a journey (and any restart you may have to take along the way) is the hardest part. Inertia can make getting started feel particularly tough. Recovery may seem impossible at first, but by harnessing the power of hope, you can achieve it.

The unknowns and uncertainties of the journey ahead can cause discomfort, fear and even paralysis. As such, you must become accustomed to being uncomfortable, worried and anxious. These are all common feelings at the start of your journey and will continue throughout. Facing these fears can only make you stronger. Remember that you have done hard things before and you can do it again. Mental illness does not take your past achievements away.

Expecting failure and negativity can hold you back, so avoid it where possible. But expect many challenges and be ready for disappointments. Things may not work out as you want them to the first, second or even third time that you embark on this journey, but you need to keep trying. Never give up. Good things eventually come to those who work hard, and it can be rewarding to take calculated risks. Find your courage within and allow yourself to be encouraged by your supporters. Do it for yourself and do it for them. Know that there is no perfect time to start and that you can't wait until you feel your absolute best. You have nothing to lose and recovery to gain.

EXERCISE

Assess your readiness for positive change and work step by step toward it. There are various tools and strategies to help instigate this change. Below are two models for evaluating your willingness to make positive changes, or whether you are already in the process of doing so.

For each, determine what stage you are at. Then, think about what you can do to move to the next stage. This may involve acquiring knowledge, learning new skills and receiving support. Consider what resources might help, including supporters and treatment providers.

Be sure to proceed with caution, slowly if necessary. Nobody reaches recovery quickly.

DARN-CAT

The acronym DARN-CAT helps assess change talk (Miller *et al.*, 2013). This stands for:

- **D**esire
- **A**bility
- **R**eason
- **N**eed
- **C**ommitment
- **A**ctivation
- **T**aking steps

Apply each to your situation and reflect.

Five Stages of Change

Another popular tool for assessing your readiness for change is the Five Stages of Change model (Prochaska *et al.*, 1983). The stages are:

1. **Precontemplation** – you are unaware of recovery
2. **Contemplation** – you want to pursue recovery, but you're uncertain about how to reach it

3. **Preparation** – you want to reach recovery and you've taken initial action toward this, such as talking to your doctor about a medication change
4. **Action** – you know you can change so you've been implementing relevant action for a while, such as taking a new prescribed medication and leading a more active life within the past six months
5. **Maintenance** – you're actively pursuing recovery in an ongoing way, for example, you've adhered to your medication for the past eight months

Apply each to your situation and reflect.

18

IDENTIFYING YOUR STRENGTHS

GOALS

Our strengths are things that we can do well, whether through natural ability or learning. Assessing your strengths can help you pursue recovery. Identify the strengths you have based on your current and past experiences, considering which ones are most helpful (or unhelpful) for your mental health recovery, as well as any that you need to improve and develop. This process will require self-awareness, but it will allow you to make better decisions moving forward and therefore help you develop the best strategies on your journey to recovery.

While most people focus on their strengths, people with mental illness often tend to focus more on their weaknesses – whether actual or perceived – due to self-doubt and a lack of self-esteem. You probably have many more strengths than you realize.

You can both enhance existing strengths and develop new ones through regular practice. This can build self-confidence, which can, in turn, enhance your strengths, making you stronger and stronger.

Testing and developing your strengths may involve stepping out of your comfort zone. In doing so, you may come to realize that some perceived weaknesses can actually be strengths in certain circumstances. Moreover, you may become aware of strengths that outsiders recognize in you that you may not have previously seen in yourself.

Don't be discouraged by any setbacks you experience while exploring your strengths. They may create new opportunities and teach valuable lessons.

You may want to move ahead quickly, but you need to find a pace that feels comfortable for you, including allowing yourself to rest from time to time. Remember that you won't always progress at the same pace, and that this is nothing to be discouraged by.

You'll need a diverse range of strengths to reach recovery. Here are a few of the most critical:

- **Self-advocacy** – speaking up for yourself
- **Hopefulness** – optimism about the future
- **Self-determination** – ability to make life choices
- **Cooperation** – ability to work with others toward a shared goal
- **Resilience** – ability to bounce back after a challenge
- **Patience** – ability to stay calm and accept delays, as there's no need to rush your journey

EXERCISE

Looking at the list below, take a little time to identify the strengths that you already have and those you need to work on. Consider how each can help you on your journey to recovery.

Accepting	Independent
Ambitious	Knowledgeable
Attentive	Objective
Brave	Open-minded
Calm	Self-motivated
Cautious	Optimistic
Confident	Patient
Committed	Persevering
Compassionate	Persistent
Consistent	Practical
Cooperative	Reasonable
Courageous	Resilient
Decisive	Resourceful
Deliberate	Responsible
Determined	Responsive
Diligent	Self-advocating
Enthusiastic	Self-determining
Fearless	Self-motivated
Flexible	Self-reliant
Focused	Sense of humor
Forgiving	Strong
Hopeful	Thorough
Imaginative	Understanding

19

GOAL-SETTING

GOALS

Small, incremental goals can build on each other, leading to ever more significant achievements and, ultimately, recovery. The most important thing about goal-setting is to make sure your goals are meaningful to you in order to keep you motivated.

Pursuing and achieving goals may require lots of effort, tools, knowledge, strength, patience and persistence. A good way to think about making and keeping goals is to name, plan, realize and reward each one that you achieve.

Start with a short list of immediate to short-term goals to avoid getting overwhelmed. Prioritize them according to "need" and "nice to have." Then, break down these goals into smaller, more manageable targets. Meanwhile, keep a list of medium- to long-term goals. Throughout this process, try to be flexible and embrace change. You may need to stop, reevaluate and change course from time to time. Be creative. Try using the S.M.A.R.T. goal approach (Drucker, 1954), which recommends making your goals:

- **S**pecific, or clear and precisely laid out. These might be things to do, not do, do less of or do more of – it's up to you.
- **M**easurable, meaning you can track your progress toward your goals. You can track these goals by time or some other measure.
- **A**greed upon, or committed to, whether with yourself or others.
- **R**ealistic, meaning they're achievable with accessible resources and under normal conditions. Unrealistic goals can lead to discouragement and worsen your health.

- **T**ime-bound, or set to be achieved with a reasonable and specific timeframe. This can protect against hurried and unsustainable action, as well as unnecessary delays and procrastination.

It's also important that you:

- Identify people who can help you reach your goals. For example, a specific accountability buddy can be very helpful.
- Anticipate challenges and develop contingency plans.
- Keep a list of your achievements handy, which you can easily review to boost your spirits.
- Celebrate when you achieve each goal, whether big or small. (External validation is nice, but internal validation matters most.)
- Always be hopeful – never give up.

EXERCISE

Knowing and addressing obstacles to achieving your goals is critical to effectively pursuing them. Internal obstacles may include self-doubt and low self-esteem. External obstacles may include lack of support, treatment options and financial resources.

- List your key obstacles. How can you address them?

- Do you need an accountability buddy? If so, who could fill this role?

- List three short-term goals. Examples may include reducing self-stigma, increasing your knowledge of your condition or seeking additional financial resources. Make sure each of these goals satisfies the 5 S.M.A.R.T. factors.

  1.

  2.

  3.

20

OVERCOMING CHALLENGES ON YOUR JOURNEY

GOALS

Challenges, setbacks, disappointments and demoralization are common features of any journey to recovery. Even if you've done everything you possibly can to prevent them, challenges will emerge, as mental illness simply is challenging. Never blame yourself for them. In fact, recovery is likely to be one of the greatest challenges you have ever taken on in your life. There's so much to do, so much to learn and so many unknowns.

However, although it won't always be smooth sailing, it's important to remember that things can and will improve. The path will become clearer along the way, you'll develop a better understanding of what helps and what doesn't. Eventually, you'll come to realize that there are no such things as mistakes – just lessons to be learned that can help you do things better the next time.

Many setbacks are the result of things you didn't know about or can't control. As such, you need to take calculated risks to move forward. This involves planning as best you can how to proceed along the way, and expecting the unexpected.

By all means, listen to the well-intentioned advice of your loved ones and healthcare providers. However, sometimes they will be too protective, which can limit your successes. Take what they say with a pinch of salt and decide on the best course for you at each stage together.

Do everything you can to experience the best outcomes. Sometimes, due to subconscious fear of success, we don't give ourselves that chance. For example, you might self-sabotage by deliberately taking actions that will lead to failure. This could be due to fear that success won't stick around for long, which will ultimately lead to disappointment; or due to an expectation of eventual failure and therefore a hope to reduce the pain of this. But there's no point in being unreasonably afraid or expecting the worst. It won't help you! Instead, try to accept that it's okay to have setbacks, and even to relapse. These things are not your fault. Yes, you may need to start over again, but each time you do so, you'll become stronger and wiser. All you can do is try your best and keep going no matter what challenges crop up along the way.

EXERCISE

Identifying challenges that we have faced in the past can help us be more prepared for obstacles that will crop up in the future. With this in mind:

- List 2 times you experienced a challenge in your mental illness recovery.

- How did you overcome these challenges?

- What challenge are you facing now about your recovery journey?

- What are some of the key risks you see in your recovery journey? What will you do if they occur?

FACING CHALLENGES

21

OBSTACLE TALK

GOALS

Unlearn your obstacles. Whenever they pop into your head, stop and try to rethink them. Are you thinking hopeless thoughts? Stop. Try being hopeful instead. Are you thinking "why bother"? Stop. Things can get better.

What about "nothing will ever change"? Stop. It's unlikely and truthfully, in some cases, they can only get better. Do you engage in negative self-talk and ruminate on distressing thoughts? Stop. Try to distract yourself – by applying a coping strategy and reframing things through a more optimistic lens, your obstacles may seem and be a little easier to overcome.

Do you focus on failures and not successes? Stop. Setbacks are nothing more than learning opportunities, and your successes probably outnumber your failures. Feeling guilt or regret for something you did while ill? Stop. Forgive yourself and try not to do it again – apologizing might help you heal. Refusing help? Stop. We all need support sometimes.

Pushing your loved ones away? Stop. They care about you and want to see you well. Not adhering to treatment? Stop. You're only hurting yourself. Self-sabotaging? Stop. Why make things worse than they already are? Comparing yourself to others? Stop. We all have different lives, and it's important to remember that everybody is struggling with something.

Thinking you'll never be the same? Stop. You can be a better and stronger person than you were. Engaging in harmful behaviors such as substance abuse? Stop. These behaviors will only make your illness worse and harder to treat. Thinking because it happened before, it will happen again? Stop. You don't have a crystal ball, and nothing is set in stone. Feeling sorry for yourself? Stop. It's disempowering. Self-pity can sap your motivation and leave you stuck in a rut. Blaming yourself for being sick? Stop. Mental illness happens to people in all walks of life and looking for someone to blame will only distract you from your recovery. Focus instead on trying as hard as you can to get well. Have a bad attitude? Definitely stop! That will stop you dead in your tracks.

Please, stop!

EXERCISE

As you reflect on each of your obstacles, think about whether they are reasonable.

When you encounter an obstacle, think about similar obstacles you've encountered in the past.

- How did you overcome them?

- What lessons did you learn that can help now?

22

UNCERTAINTY

GOALS

Uncertainty in life is a certainty whether you're well or not. It can cause a tremendous amount of anxiety and emotional distress. "What is my condition?" "Will these medications work?" "How long will I be sick?" "Will I relapse?" Nobody knows these things for certain – not even the best doctors. "Will I ever get better?" Maybe you can, but if you don't work hard to get well, you'll remove all doubt – that's a certainty.

Lots of people with mental illness struggle with uncertainty. This is extremely common and nothing to be ashamed of. We all sometimes feel like we have no control over our lives. Others may step in and try to take control away from us. They may think they know best. This can make us feel hopeless, helpless, afraid, frustrated and angry. However, the sooner you accept that there are some situations you can't control, the better. This will allow you to focus on the things you can control.

You can try to minimize the adverse consequences of uncertainties by expecting, planning for and being ready to act on them. In doing so, you can take back some sense of control and make distressing situations a lot easier to manage. How we react to uncertainty can be more impactful than the uncertainty itself. You can learn a lot from how you dealt with past uncertainties – try to remember what did and didn't help at the time.

Reaching out for help can be useful. Never surrender to uncertainties – you have to keep trying your best, and doing what you can to remain optimistic. Learn which coping strategies work best for you in times of uncertainty. Many people find spirituality helpful. Even just telling yourself that things will work out can help you to cope with uncertainly – doing so may give you the motivation you need to make things work out. Another effective coping strategy is taking stock of the things you're grateful for in life (this is called making a "gratitude list"). Crucially, remember that uncertainty doesn't always have to lead to the worst-case scenario – it could just as easily lead to the best-case scenario.

If you're feeling uncertain, always think: "What's the best that can happen?"

EXERCISE

Let's create your coping strategy list. List 10 things that you're grateful for, a reminder that can help you when you're uncertain. Return to this list when you are feeling anxious or distressed.

My coping strategies:

1.

2.

3.

4.

5.

6.

7.

8.

9.

10.

23

DISCOURAGEMENT

GOALS

The journey to recovery can be a long one, and it's inevitable that, along the way, things will go wrong. Things will also go right. Learn to expect both over time. This is part of life, with or without mental illness. It's natural to feel disappointed if you're not getting as well (or doing so as quickly) as you'd like. Being discouraged, frustrated or heartbroken are all natural responses. Go ahead and cry. Go ahead and scream. Release your emotions – this is healthy.

If they're okay with it, vent about your concerns to a loved one, but try not to complain. Your loved one has experienced disappointments in life too. Everyone has. They may be more empathetic than you think. You may want to give up, be ambivalent, stop caring about yourself or experience hopelessness and helplessness. A lot of this may be due to the uncertainties stemming from your illness. You have to accept the uncertainty, but you must always hold on to hope.

Faith, including religious belief and spiritualism, helps millions of people worldwide cope with uncertainty. You've got to believe that things will not feel nor be this bad forever, and that better days lie ahead. Trying to control something you simply can't can be exhausting. Instead, focus on what you can control and do something about it. Whatever you do, the worst response is to lie in bed or on the couch all day, to stay locked up in your home, withdrawn and isolated. You have overcome challenges in the past and can do it again. Remember that.

Think of all your accomplishments – mental illness does not and cannot take those away from you. Just living with mental illness is an accomplishment in itself – be proud of that. When your friends and family tell you how well you are doing, that they are proud of you, believe them. If you've been fighting your illness, stop. It can needlessly delay your recovery. Know that you can happily co-exist with your illness. It's okay to take a break and even fall into a slump from time to time, but you must get back up on your feet and carry on.

EXERCISE

- What is discouraging you from your path to recovery right now?

- How can you address this? What can you control to make things better?

- Who can help you get motivated?

- What are five things you can do to make you feel better when you feel discouraged? List them below.

    1.

    2.

    3.

    4.

    5.

24

ASKING FOR HELP

GOALS

Asking for help can be hard and requires courage. However, try to remember that it is a sign of strength – not weakness. Never be ashamed or embarrassed about your struggles. When it comes to reaching out, there are a few things you should think about. Firstly, you need to be able to identify when you need help – it is always better to do so sooner rather than later.

If you find yourself struggling, let a loved one know you need help. You may be worried about being a burden, but chances are they will be relieved that you asked for help instead of waiting until things got worse. They will worry less if they know you're trying to take the best care of yourself possible, and will likely be empathetic and understanding. Don't assume otherwise. Your pride can also get in the way of asking for help, especially when you believe you should be able to address the situation on your own. However, people who care for you will want to help you.

Ask for the help you think you need. Your loved ones can help you think about this. Ask them for their suggestions – and be receptive to what they say. They may be able to help you, but sometimes the best support they can give you will be to help you get the help you really need. It's good to know who can help best in any given situation. This may be a loved one, but it could also be a healthcare provider.

Sometimes it's good to have a few people to turn to for help. You can have a supporter that helps you with treatment and another supporter that you simply spend time with. Just having people there for you can be comforting and reduce some of the uncertainty of mental illness. Always try to demonstrate your appreciation to supporters. A simple thank you can be extremely meaningful to those who care about you.

Most importantly, ask yourself if you're doing everything you can to help yourself.

EXERCISE

- What do you need help with?

- Who are the best people to help you with what you need? This could be a loved one, a friend, a clergy person, a co-worker, a community member, etc.

- What can these people help you with? This could involve helping you research treatment options, accompanying you to a session, providing transportation or even just listening.

25

SHARING YOUR STORY

GOALS

Sharing your story with the right people can help your mental health. Conversely, not disclosing or "hiding" your mental illness can lead to significant emotional distress down the line. You might also make counter-productive and incorrect presumptions about other people, which may lead you to withdraw and isolate, feel ashamed and embarrassed, or lose supporters. However, while being open about your illness can be relieving, it requires careful consideration. The most important thing is that you are comfortable with the decision.

If done thoughtfully, sharing can lead to personal growth, better care, support and connectivity, greater authenticity, improved self-esteem, empowerment and pride. You don't need to share every detail about your condition and you should only come out to people with whom you feel comfortable sharing. However, most people will likely be more empathetic and understanding than you expect.

Bear in mind that there are risks too. Sharing your struggles with mental illness may cause you to experience stigma, lose friendships, receive unhelpful and hurtful advice, and even face discrimination in areas such as the workplace. However, with the proper preparation, you can minimize the possible adverse consequences. Those who come out usually start with a few friends and family members. You may learn that many people you know have mental illness too. Many will likely want to support you, which will be more effective if you let them know how.

Make this an ongoing dialogue, as there may be a lot to share, and you can't let it all out in one discussion. Also, when you spend time with people, you shouldn't feel the need always to talk about how you're feeling. Sometimes it can help to not talk about it and focus on other things. Publicly sharing your experiences can help create greater awareness and understanding of mental illness. You can even inspire hope in others and become an advocate on issues affecting people with mental illness. This can make you feel more connected to others and give you a sense of belonging to a community.

There are many places to share your story, including support groups, social media, blogs, academic journals, books, arts, public speaking and advocacy work. Remember that you have something inspiring to share and others are interested in what you have to say.

EXERCISE

What's your story? Write a brief paragraph describing what's most important about your history and identity, including your mental illness. This "script" may help you prepare to share your story with others. Remember that you are in control of your story.

- Whom would you like to share your story with first?

- Who are the people who could benefit most from hearing your story?

- What are your hesitations about sharing your story?

26

EMBRACE HAPPINESS

GOALS

Finding meaning and purpose in life can give you happiness and a sense of satisfaction. Think about what made you happy in the past. The pursuit of happiness can be a strong motivator to getting well – it can inspire hope and optimism and boost self-esteem. Most importantly, it can help you appreciate life.

However, you may not have been happy for a while, or you might even feel like you will never be happy again. If you are happy now, you may be afraid that it won't last and you'll be hurt again soon. These are not uncommon fears. Reliving old times through people, places and things can trigger happy memories. It's nice to do so in the company of old friends. Sometimes they can better recall how happy you were in the past, because when you're feeling sad it might be hard to recall these memories. They can help you realize that you were happy before and can be again.

Looking through old photos and videos can help too. Mental illness can't take away these happy memories, just as it can't take away your ability to be happy again in the future, but it can make it harder to find happiness during your struggles. Think about what makes you happy now, even if it isn't much. Identify these things and try to build on them. Think of what might make you happy in the future and plan for it. You must always give happiness a chance – you can't dismiss the thought with a frown of disbelief. Instead, try (or even force) a smile. Better still, laugh a little. Just being silly can sometimes be enough to help. Let your loved ones try to make you happy, do things that you enjoyed before you became unwell. Being happy again does not necessarily mean returning to your former self but embracing your new self with new possibilities. It means realizing you can live with a mental illness and still be happy.

EXERCISE

Explore things big and small that might give you moments of happiness.

- What made you happy in the past?

- What makes you happy now?

- Who is the best person to lift your mood right now?

- What activities can you try to lift your mood?

27

POSITIVE PSYCHOLOGY

GOALS

Positive psychology is the study of strengths and positive emotions that can occur during times of adversity. They can help you overcome challenges, build resilience and live a meaningful life. Positive emotions include joy, gratitude, serenity, interest, hope, pride, amusement, inspiration, awe and love. These feelings may significantly lower emotional distress, even in the face of challenges.

The Broaden-and-Build Theory states that positive emotions can "promote discovery of novel and creative actions, ideas and social bonds, which in turn build that individual's personal resources," which can lead to helpful skill development (Fredrickson *et al.*, 2004). Thinking and acting creatively is about not limiting yourself to the norms. It's about calculated risk-taking to find the best path for you. This can be hard, because a lot of people respond to mental illness conservatively. They can discourage outside-the-box approaches, but sometimes challenging the odds can lead to positive outcomes.

Post-traumatic growth is another positive-psychology concept, which you may find hopeful. "Post-traumatic growth is the experience of positive change that occurs as a result of the struggle with highly challenging life crises. These changes include an increased appreciation for life in general, more meaningful interpersonal relationships, an increased sense of personal strength, changed priorities, and a richer existential and spiritual life" (Tedeschi, 2009).

Now may be the time for you to reflect on what your struggles have taught you about your life. You may realize that the way you were living contributed to your illness. You may be grateful that your life did not turn out to be what you expected. It is important to remember that returning to your former self may not be your only or best option. Adversity can help you grow and make you strong enough to take on new challenges. It can lead you to a better life than you thought would ever be possible.

EXERCISE

If you are struggling right now, try to think of this as an opportunity to learn and become stronger.

- Think back on prior periods of struggle and adversity. Be proud of yourself for coming out the other side. What skills or positive emotions helped you in those challenging times? What new strengths did you develop in the process?

- Are there any role models or people you admire who demonstrated strength through periods of adversity?

28

GRATITUDE

GOALS

Gratitude is a form of recognition, a sense of thankfulness and happiness about the people and things that are good in your life. It can counter the negativity we so often focus on. Feeling grateful can often be difficult for people struggling with mental illness. Sometimes, it's all too easy to focus on the illness and miss out on the things you should be thankful for.

You may be extremely angry. You may think you have nothing good in your life and tell people just that, which can be hurtful to both of you. Mental illness can blind you to the good things in your life. We can't take for granted things like access to good healthcare, housing and the support of a loved one. Know that there's always something to be grateful for, even if may seem small and insignificant.

We need to reframe the negative into the positive, and gratitude can help us put challenges and setbacks into perspective. You can feel strong emotions about your illness, but still be grateful. Some people may say that you're ungrateful or don't appreciate them – maybe this is true, but it's more likely that it isn't. Statements like this can be hurtful and make you feel guilty. It can be difficult to show gratitude when you're sick and don't care about anything, but it's important to show your supporters gratitude and apologize if you have not. A little thank you or sign of appreciation can make a relationship stronger and better and can make you feel better about yourself in the process.

Gratitude is not some innate quality that exists separately from your circumstances and experiences – it's about seeing the good in what you have. It can help counter negativity and make you feel better, happier and more optimistic about life. Positive emotions can also be triggered by savoring, which is being aware and appreciating what's good in life as it happens. So take some time and notice the little things you have to be grateful for.

EXERCISE

Let's create your gratitude list! List 10 things you are grateful for. Return to this list when you are feeling anxious or distressed.

What I am grateful for:

1.

2.

3.

4.

5.

6.

7.

8.

9.

10.

MANAGING EMOTIONS

29

TRIGGERS

GOALS

A trigger, often referred to as a stressor, is an action or situation that can result in an adverse emotional reaction. This can, in turn, cause symptoms to resurface or worsen. Addressing potential triggers before they appear can often be easier than dealing with the fallout afterwards. Triggers are individualized experiences that vary widely from person to person. A trigger may elicit a physical reaction, such as heavy breathing, or an emotional reaction, such as feeling disrespected. It may cause a wide range of emotions, such as anger, which can be detrimental to mental health. Some people may say that we're overreacting or "too sensitive" when triggered, which can be upsetting and feel invalidating.

Many different stimuli can act as triggers, and they are often strongly tied to past experiences. External triggers, such as interpersonal conflicts, are common. For example, reading or hearing about things like suicide or self-injury could be triggering. Internal triggers are often feelings that cause an emotional response – for example, becoming angry when you think someone is making fun of you. Trauma triggers remind you of a previous traumatic event, while symptom triggers might include disrupted sleep, which can be very bad for your mental health.

It's important to identify triggers, make a plan for addressing them, try problem-focused and emotional-focused coping, communicate to those who may be triggering you, pick the right therapy, reality-check your thoughts, look out for trigger warnings and practice self-care. It's difficult to control our triggers; however, we can apply what we have learned from past experiences to manage and limit the risk of being re-triggered. We can't diminish or dismiss the trigger, or only focus on what happens after we're triggered – we must also focus on what we can do beforehand. We might even be able to prevent the trigger by anticipating it. In doing so, we can have some control, and anything that gives us a little control over our mental illness can help keep us well.

EXERCISE

- Describe your top two triggers. Detail the who, what, where, when and why of these triggers.

- How can you try to address your triggers?

- Do your supporters know your triggers? What do you want your supporters to know about your triggers or do if they think you've become triggered? Tell your supporters in advance what you would like them to do if they think you're triggered or behaving unusually.

30

THOUGHTS

GOALS

Thoughts are your opinions about yourself, other people and things. They can be automatic, habitual, repeated or progressive. They may be spontaneous or otherwise quickly derived. Thoughts can sometimes be unsubstantiated, negative and unreasonable. They are usually triggered by an event or situation, and can themselves be triggering. Triggering thoughts may be based on unfounded assumptions, misinterpretations or misunderstandings. They can lead to significant emotional distress and other adverse consequences, such as strained personal relationships.

These thoughts should be addressed as quickly as possible because they may intensify over time. Self-care interventions can help you cope with negative thoughts. These actions may include mindfulness or focusing on the present moment, which can be particularly helpful for managing ruminations.

Repeated exposure to negative thoughts may cause them to worsen, and may even lead to physical reactions, particularly stress. This can cause your negative thoughts to spiral out of control. Wherever possible, try to resist the temptation to address negative thoughts immediately. Know that addressing thoughts constructively may take time. Set a timeframe in the near future to address them after the initial emotional distress has passed, which will allow for a more thoughtful response.

The best way to address negative thoughts is to test if they are reasonable. Consider if negative thoughts are "cognitive distortions", or irrational thoughts or beliefs (Beck, 2021). Challenge your thoughts – consider the evidence for and against them. Are there alternative explanations for what is happening or how you are feeling? The objective in doing this is to eliminate or minimize the adverse impacts of thoughts. Try talking to a therapist or trusted supporter about your triggers and negative thoughts. Some people with mental illness are more vulnerable to negative thinking because of the challenges they have faced in the past, but the past need not dictate the present or the future. When you find yourself thinking negatively, stop and catch yourself – these thought patterns can only cause needless pain and distress.

EXERCISE

- Do you have triggers that cause you to think any of the following thoughts?

I feel annoyed.	I feel like a loser.
I feel ashamed.	I feel lonely.
I feel attacked.	I feel offended.
I felt blamed.	I feel overwhelmed.
I feel controlled.	I feel powerless.
I felt defeated.	I feel rejected.
I feel disappointed.	I feel scared.
I feel disrespected.	I feel stupid.
I feel embarrassed.	I feel stressed.
I feel envious.	I feel threatened.
I feel exhausted.	I feel trapped.
I feel excluded.	I feel uncared for.
I feel forgotten.	I feel uncomfortable.
I feel frustrated.	I feel unfairness.
I feel helpless.	I feel unhappy.
I feel hopeless.	I feel unloved.
I feel hurt.	I feel unsure.
I feel ignored.	I feel worried.
I feel insecure.	I feel victimized.
I feel judged.	

- Are there actions you can take to avoid these triggers and thoughts?

31

REALITY TESTING

GOALS

Reality testing means ensuring that your subjective experience of the world matches the objective external reality. Doing so can save you a lot of grief. Try asking yourself: "Is there evidence that supports my current conclusion?" Consider the reasonableness of your interpretation from as many angles as possible. Maybe your interpretation of the facts is based on a misunderstanding – yours or someone else's. Are you giving people the benefit of the doubt when their conclusion can be readily disproven?

Avoid doubting clear explanations. Stick with the facts. It's important to stay in the present moment. Focus on the current situation and not some future theoretical possibility. Carefully and thoughtfully consider the situation, preferably when you are not in a state of emotional distress, if possible. Remember that your current state of mind may be influencing your interpretation of the facts. When you find yourself doubting your experience of external reality, it can be very useful to consider past events. Have you experienced the same thoughts before? Was your interpretation reasonable? Are you allowing your preconceptions to distort your thinking?

Talk to people who were there when the event occurred. They may possess a more objective view or have information you don't. Try reframing your interpretation of the facts from the negative to the positive. To help do so, write down all the facts you have gathered so they are all in view. Create a list of possible interpretations, making sure to include at least one positive interpretation. Imagine that you are a third party and rank each of the interpretations based on the facts on a scale of 1 (highly reasonable) to 5 (unreasonable). Try this with a therapist or a trusted supporter as the third party as well. Consider their interpretation of the evidence. Everyone can view situations differently, so it can be helpful to hear different opinions.

Think of the consequences of unreasonably interpreting events or jumping to conclusions. Your sensitivity may influence your interpretation. It is important to remember that a lot of people with mental illness are hypersensitive due to self-stigma. Facts are facts, but their interpretation can vary from person-to-person.

Basing your interpretation of events on facts will allow you to more constructively address events that may re-trigger you. We live in reality, so reality is what we should go with. Reality test your facts.

EXERCISE

To test the reasonableness of a thought, ask yourself if it reflects some type of cognitive distortion (Beck, 2021), such as:

1. **Black-or-white thinking** – only thinking in extremes, instead of shades of gray
2. **Blame** – blaming yourself for something you can't entirely control
3. **Catastrophizing** – assuming the worst-case scenario
4. **Crystal-ball thinking** – jumping to conclusions
5. **Focusing on the bad** – lingering on the negative aspects of the situation while dismissing the positives
6. **Mind-reading** – jumping to conclusions based on what you imagine others are thinking
7. **Overgeneralizing** – arriving at a conclusion based on one example
8. **Rejecting the positive** – attributing a positive to luck rather than merit
9. **"Should" statements** – focusing on what should have happened instead of accepting what has happened
10. **Unfounded assumptions** – assuming negative emotions reflect the truth

32

FEELINGS

GOALS

Triggers can lead to thoughts that might arouse distinct feelings. Feelings are subjective thoughts, which can be pleasant or unpleasant. They may be unnoticed, insignificant, minimal or extensive, and can last for a long time or be gone in an instant.

Try to remember that the event itself is not as important to your mental wellbeing as your interpretation of the event. Fear and anger can be the most harmful feelings. Others include uncertainty, worry, helplessness, frustration, hopelessness, pessimism and sadness. These can be difficult to control and are often interconnected. Anger, for example, is often rooted in fear, which is often rooted in uncertainty.

It can be helpful to try to identify and manage these underlying triggers, thoughts and feelings. Ask yourself: "Are my feelings appropriate or disproportionate to the triggering event?" Comforting supporters, therapy, coping strategies and self-care can help address negative feelings. Consider how likely or unlikely it is that the outcome you fear will come to be. Think of past experiences where you needlessly worried and try not to overanalyze underlying triggers or predict their outcomes.

It is important not to surrender to your feelings or impulsively act on them. However, you shouldn't bottle them up either, as this can cause them to intensify. It's important to address your feelings because otherwise they may hurt your mental health and even lead to physical concerns such as sleep disruption. Remember that, even when your feelings may not be "reasonable," they are valid. At the same time, remember that feelings are not facts.

On the flip side, some feelings are good. When we start to feel well, it can be like an awakening. We may become excited about life and experience some intense feelings. Don't be afraid of these. Don't let your loved ones try to subdue you when you are in control of yourself, for fear that your excitement might lead you to become unwell or set you up for disappointment.

Embrace your passion and live life fully. Feelings can be bad or good – accepting the bad and encouraging the good will significantly help you on the road to recovery.

EXERCISE

By monitoring your feelings and moods daily, you may be able to identify patterns that can help you toward the goal of recovery.

- Identify the three feelings you most frequently struggle with and rank their intensity using a 10-point scale (1 to 10 from the worst to the best you've ever felt).

    1.

    2.

    3.

- Identify ways you can address these feelings. What has worked in the past?

- Reward yourself for improving your feelings or mood.

- If you are worried or anxious right now, identify one helpful positive thought.

33

ANGER

GOALS

Anger can be one of the most destructive feelings. You may be angry for many reasons, including your mental illness, the feeling that you aren't getting better, unpleasant side effects of medications, caregivers that don't seem to understand what you're going through and insensitive friends. You may be angry at yourself for getting sick. Self-loathing is common and nothing to be ashamed of. You may want to blame others, such as loved ones, treatment providers or even God. Many underlying feelings manifest themselves as anger, including loss of control, uncertainty, frustration, mistreatment, hopelessness and helplessness, among others.

You might express this anger through destructive behavior, such as substance abuse or hurtful fights. You might project your own emotions onto someone else. Anger can manifest itself in spontaneous outbursts during moments of frustration, which you may regret later. This can be harmful and hurtful. Remember, while venting can help, complaining and blaming usually won't. It can be helpful to let your loved ones know how angry your illness makes you feel. However, try not to personalize what they do or say out of ignorance. Being ill is nothing you nor anyone else did to you, and you can't let it destroy your relationships.

You and your loved ones must turn mental illness into the enemy – not each other. Mental illness happens, but you needn't feel helpless against any anger you experience as a result. By effectively applying coping strategies, you can regain some control. These can range from calming strategies that can disarm your anger to vigorous ones like intense exercise that allows you to release pent up energy. Everyone has different coping strategies that work best.

You may not be able to control all of your triggers, but you can learn how to more easily control how you manage your feelings. It may be difficult to accept your mental illness, but it is important to try your best given the circumstances. On a positive note, anger may be a strong motivating force. Act on it constructively.

EXERCISE

Sometimes our feelings are repeatedly triggered by the same circumstances. In these cases, it can be helpful to keep a record of your feelings and try to identify patterns. Whenever you experience a recurring negative feeling, try asking yourself the following questions:

- What was the trigger?

- What was I doing?

- Who was I with?

- When did it happen?

- Where was I?

- What were my thoughts?

- What were my feelings?

- What was my reaction?

- What can I do to better manage my reaction in future?

34

DEPRESSION

GOALS

Depression in the everyday sense is different from depression as an illness. Many people with mental illness experience some form of depression. This can adversely impact how you feel, think and act. At times, it can cause intense feelings of sadness and loss of interest in activities you once enjoyed. It can affect your sleep, energy and motivation.

"Everyday depression" may be triggered by an unpleasant event such as an upsetting experience. Once resolved, you may feel better. At other times, depression can surface inexplicably, even at times when things are going well. This can be incredibly discouraging, and may lead you to feel like, no matter what, you'll always feel depressed.

In times like this, it can make it hard to get anything done. Even getting up out of bed can seem impossible, and doing nothing can make you even more depressed. It can lead to a downward spiral, where everyday depression becomes the illness of depression. Demoralization (frustration when many bad things happen) can also turn into depression. It may cause you to isolate, withdraw and be unable to leave your home. You may experience intense, overwhelming and unrelenting emotional distress and rumination.

At this point, it may feel like no one you speak to and nothing you try can make you feel better. At times, you may even feel like you can't go on. These moments can be particularly dangerous and you must reach out for help immediately, because depression can get worse over time. Address it quickly.

A variety of coping strategies might help you, especially distractions, which may calm the ruminating thoughts that usually make depression worse. Medications and therapy may be able to help you. When you're in this state, speak to your loved ones – push yourself to do more, even if it's the bare minimum. Overcoming depression alone is difficult, so ask for help. You don't need to suffer alone.

EXERCISE

Get to know your early warning signs for depression. To help yourself do so, note the following characteristics of your depressive episodes.

- Triggers: What causes it?

- Emotions: How do I feel?

- Activities: What changes?

- Duration: How quickly do episodes come on and how long do they last?

Share these indicators with loved ones and supporters and healthcare providers. Ask yourself:

- What is my action plan for addressing my depression?

- Tell your loved ones and supporters in advance what you would like them to do if they notice any of your depression indicators.

TREATMENT

35

MENTAL HEALTH EDUCATION

GOALS

It is important to know as much as you can about your illness, but it can sometimes be difficult to step back and view your own situation through an objective lens. However, even learning a little can help. It can make you feel empowered, more in control and less uncertain about your condition, allowing you to be more proactive about treatment and take better care of yourself.

It can also make you a better patient and enhance your treatment with your healthcare provider. Equipped with this knowledge, you will be better able to identify issues which you can talk to your healthcare provider about. A few key things to learn include: risk factors and triggers, warning signs, symptoms, treatment options and crisis interventions. You should also try to learn about general good mental health strategies such as stress management and self-care activities and how to incorporate them into your daily life.

Having this knowledge can help you take more responsibility for your illness and play a more active role in your care through illness self-management. You are the best expert when it comes to you and you know best your wants and needs, but education and good care can help you make the best decisions. You'll also learn that you're not alone – 20% of people are living with a mental illness (National Alliance on Mental Illness, n.d.).

Knowing more about mental illness can help you realize that you're not a problem, failure or loser just for having an illness. In addition to healthcare professionals, education sources can include peers with mental illness and mental health non-profits. While the internet can be a useful resource, always be careful about what you read online. Good online sources of information include the websites for the American Psychiatric Association, National Alliance on Mental Illness, Mayo Clinic, Healthline, WebMD and SMI Advisor.

Always verify information, especially treatment-related information, with your healthcare provider before acting on it. Your loved ones may also want to learn about your condition in order to help you. Be open to the advice of loved ones and treatment providers. Ideally, you, your loved ones and treatment providers should be sharing knowledge with each other.

EXERCISE

- What do you know about your condition?

- What more would you like to learn more about in regard to your condition?

- What additional sources of information and education about your mental illness will you access?

- What questions do you have for your doctor or treatment provider?

- Have you talked to other people with mental illness? Is there a peer you can turn to for more information on their experience? You can find peers at ForLikeMinds.com.

36

THERAPY

GOALS

Therapy is a great tool for helping you understand and manage your feelings. It provides an opportunity to speak candidly to a trained, objective professional about your concerns. They may be better equipped to help you than your loved ones. Therapists can include licensed mental health counselors, social workers, psychologists and psychiatrists. Therapy plus medication can be the most effective treatment strategy. However, choosing a therapist is a major decision, and before doing so you should select a few candidates and carefully vet them. Length and type of experience are important considerations to take into account when choosing the right therapist for you.

Moreover, it's important to learn about different types of therapy before subscribing to one. Three of the most popular types of therapy are: psychodynamic therapy, cognitive behavioral therapy (CBT) and dialectical behavioral therapy (DBT).

Psychodynamic therapy focuses on the "psychological roots of emotional suffering through self-reflection and self-examination, and patient-therapist relationship" (American Psychological Association, 2010). Cognitive behavioral therapy "helps people identify their distressing thoughts and evaluate how realistic the thoughts are and how to address them" (Beck Institute, n.d.). Dialectical behavioral therapy helps individuals learn to regulate and tolerate their emotions (Behavioral Tech, n.d.). Next, consider your "interpersonal fit" with the therapist, based on your wants and needs.

Carefully consider the qualities you would like in a therapist. You may need to try a few before you find one you like.

If your budget allows, try to have a couple of sessions with each candidate. In some cases, you may like the fit, but not the advice. Be sure to consider why you don't and talk about it. A culturally competent therapist may better appreciate the influences of your particular community and background. At the beginning of therapy, it can be helpful to identify your concerns and goals for therapy. These may change over time, so you may need to reassess your choice in the future. It's difficult to predict how long it will take to see good results. Try to be patient, and remember that it's important to talk about your feelings instead of bottling things up.

EXERCISE

Below are a few ideal traits in therapists and psychiatrists.

- Which of these describe what you want in a therapist?

- Which of these are missing in your current therapist?

Empathetic	Does not make you feel defensive
Compassionate	Non-accusatory
Comforting	Treats as a person
Understanding	Helps emotional growth
Sensitive	Good listener
Respectful	Engages in conversation
Patient	Encourage feedback
Does not make me feel intimidated	Honest and truthful
	Respects your privacy
Validates concerns	Help gain perspective
Genuine	Educates you
Unbiased	Helps you set goals
Non-stigmatizing	Leaves you feeling good after sessions
Non-judgmental	
Culturally competent	Gets it

37

PSYCHIATRIC TREATMENT

GOALS

Psychiatric treatment typically includes medication as a central component. It may also include therapy. A prescriber collaborates with a patient to establish a medication regimen, prescribes medication and manages the regimen. They can be a primary care provider, psychiatric nurse practitioner or psychiatrist. Medication can be critical to reaching recovery, but it is often more effective when taken in combination with therapy.

It can be helpful for your prescriber to collaborate with your non-prescribing treatment providers as well as your primary care provider on physical health matters. The best way to find a good prescriber may be through a referral from a trusted person, especially a person you know who is currently in treatment or has been in the past. There are a few online directories you can consult, such as *Psychology Today*. Select a few prescribers and review their qualifications, including education, board certifications, expertise, affiliations, publications and years of experience. It is also important to consider "fit," which can be one of the most important factors for treatment success.

You may have to try a few prescribers before you find the right one for you, and that's okay. It may be helpful to bring a family member or friend with whom you feel comfortable to a first appointment to help raise relevant questions. Treatment approach is extremely important – some prescribers may only focus on symptoms, problems, deficits or diagnoses. Good treatment should be person-centered and strengths-based. For some prescribers, stability is the primary treatment goal. However, a better goal is remission, which is the point at which your symptoms are no longer of clinical relevance.

Controlling your symptoms is a critical step toward recovery. It is important that you find a prescriber with whom you are comfortable, as the process requires close collaboration. Your prescriber should treat you to help you reach recovery. Most crucially, prescribers should always have hope for you no matter how much and how long you've struggled. Make sure you choose the best prescriber for you.

EXERCISE

The following questions and discussion topics may help you evaluate a prescriber or potential "fit" and consider other treatment issues.

- What is your treatment approach?

- What is your diagnosis and prognosis for me?

- I would like to discuss my treatment goals.

- I would like to discuss how my treatment goals can help me achieve my life goals.

- I would like to develop a care plan.

- Who do you think should be part of my care plan?

- I would like to develop a crisis plan.

- Do you recommend therapy?

- What type of therapy do you recommend for me?

38

MEDICATION

GOALS

In order to live in recovery, most people dealing with mental illness need some form of medication. The systematic "trial and error" approach, which is often required to find the best treatments for you, can be extremely frustrating and discouraging. However, it's important to remain patient and not give up, because most people eventually find a regimen that works. Prior to embarking on a course of medication, it can be helpful to weigh the pros and cons of each drug with your prescriber.

If a medication helps but has side effects, you need to decide if you're willing to live with them. If you are having medication side effects, you may be able to address them more easily than you think by discussing them with your prescriber. You may be able to take an alternative medication, reduce your dose or take a supplementary medication to address the side effect. Taking more than one medication is more common than you might think.

You may need to accept that you'll need to be on medication for the rest of your life to stay well – this is nothing to be ashamed of, and is no different than being on medication for diabetes or high blood pressure. If you stop a medication without supervision by your prescriber, you may put yourself at high risk of relapse or withdrawal symptoms. Try to avoid taking drastic action like this, but make sure to have a say in your care. Doing so can be highly empowering and can encourage you to take greater control of your illness and your recovery moving forward.

Shared decision-making is an evidence-based approach to work with your doctor and take more responsibility for your condition. Your prescriber will use their expertise to offer you medication options and will let you decide what you want to take. The right medication can help you live the life you want. However, if medicines have been unsuccessful, there are many non-medication treatments such as electroconvulsive therapy (ECT) and newer forms of brain stimulation that can often help. Sometimes, specific forms of psychotherapy like DBT can also work when medicines don't help. Never lose hope – the right treatment plan for you is out there.

EXERCISE

Below are a few medication questions for you to discuss with your prescriber. They may help you and your prescriber determine what the best options are for you.

- How can you treat my condition?

- What are my medication options?

- Can you explain each medication option to me?

- What are the side effects of the medication? How can I tell if a side effect is actually a symptom?

- Will these medications have any impact on my physical health? Will there be any activity restrictions?

- Can I safely take these medications with the medications I am taking for my other health conditions?

- How long will it take for the medication to be effective?

- What's the best way to stop medication?

- What's the best way to reduce my dose?

- Can you recommend ways I can save money on medications?

Below are some tips to help you adhere to your medication treatment:

- Make them part of your daily routine.
- Simplify your regimen.
- Recognize and proactively manage potential side effects.
- Learn about them from reputable sources.
- Know your treatment goals.
- Know the consequences of not taking them.

39

HEALTH COMORBIDITIES

GOALS

Comorbidities refer to the presence of two or more conditions in one person. Comorbidity of mental illnesses is common, such as having depression and anxiety. A skilled healthcare provider should be able to treat both at the same time and/or be able to refer you to other provider(s) who can help. It is also common to have a mental illness and substance use disorder and/ or physical health conditions. These additional conditions may trigger or worsen a mental illness and make it harder to treat. As such, it is essential to disclose all of your mental health, substance use and physical health challenges to all of your providers.

People sometimes self-medicate with substances, which can be extremely harmful. Integrated treatment of mental illness and substance use is considered best practice. There are providers that specialize in the treatment of substance use and helpful support groups.

Comorbidity of mental illness and physical health conditions is also common. Sometimes it may not be clear if a physical problem reflects a comorbid medical condition or a medication side effect. For example, many medications can sometimes cause weight gain, which can lead to obesity. This can place a person at high risk for several diseases, notably type 2 diabetes. Medications may also cause sedation, which can impair concentration and contribute to a sedentary lifestyle, which may make it more difficult to pursue your life goals. Be sure to talk to your doctor about any concerns you may have because they can sometimes be addressed.

A poor diet, such as eating too many processed foods, can also affect your mood. Many people with mental illness smoke excessively, which can lead to a wide range of health issues, including heart disease and, ultimately, a reduced life span. It's important for your psychiatrist and primary care doctor to collaborate on treatment, especially medication management, as medications for different conditions may have important drug interactions. As such, getting an annual checkup is good practice. Remember, you are a whole person – you need to take care of both your mental and physical health.

EXERCISE

- If you use substances, consider the pros and cons. How do you feel after the positive effects have worn off?

- If you suffer from physical health conditions, the doctors that manage your mental and physical health should be collaborating with you. Are they?

If you have a substance use or physical health condition, you can consult the following resources for help addressing them: American Academy of Addiction Psychiatry, Alcoholics Anonymous, Narcotics Anonymous, American Diabetes Association, American Lung Association and Choose My Plate.

40

SUICIDE AWARENESS

GOALS

If you find yourself experiencing suicidal thoughts or engaging in suicidal ideation, **it is vital that you reach out for help, whether to a trusted friend, a family member, a healthcare provider, 988, a crisis hotline or 911**. Remember, help is available, and you are never alone. In these moments, think of all the wonderful people in your life, how much they care for you and how much you care for them. Think of all of the people, pets and special things you would be leaving behind.

Things may get hard from time to time, but they can and will get better. You have many things to live for, but sometimes our pain can blind us to this. Know that people love you and need you in their lives. Being aware of warning signs of suicide can help you know when you need to reach out for help. These might include the things you think, feel, say and do.

According to the American Foundation for Suicide Prevention (AFSP, n.d.), watch out for:

1. Talk of being a burden to others, killing yourself, experiencing unbearable pain, having no reason to live or feeling trapped
2. Moods that include loss of interest, depression, irritability, anxiety, humiliation or rage
3. Behavior changes such as increased substance use, withdrawal and isolation, sleep changes, saying goodbye, giving away possessions, writing a suicide note or acting recklessly
4. Looking for a way to end your life

If you've had suicidal thoughts, remove any weapons from your home and ask a trusted person to hold your medicines if needed. In these scenarios, you must get the help you need QUICKLY, even if that means spending a few days in a hospital. Living with mental illness can be overwhelming and highly discouraging at times, but recovery is possible, and that's an important reason for living on.

You have so much waiting for you in the future, and many of your best days are yet to come. Suicide sacrifices long-term possibilities to fix a short-term situation. Please remember – asking for help is a sign of strength. You are stronger than you think.

EXERCISE

If you are experiencing suicidal thoughts, it is important you reach out for help. This help can take many forms, some of which are listed below (for readers based outside the US, please see the Mental Health Resources section):

- Speak to a trusted friend or family member.
- Speak to your healthcare provider.
- Call 988 Suicide and Crisis Lifeline.
- Call 911.
- Contact the Crisis Text Line. To do so, text "HOME" TO 741741.

A suicide attempt is an action someone takes in an effort to end their life. This is different from non-suicidal self-injury (NSSI), where people may try to hurt themselves but not cause their death. However, NSSI is a risk factor for future suicide attempts and should be taken extremely seriously.

- Have you ever had suicidal thoughts?

- Have you ever made a suicide attempt?

- What were the triggers?

- What are your key reasons for living? Note that recovery is a reason for living.

41

CRISIS PLANNING

GOALS

Crisis planning can be critical, empowering and even lifesaving. It can help remove some of the uncertainty you may be feeling and can allow you to retain some control during a crisis. Try talking about and developing a plan with loved ones and healthcare providers. Consider preparing a Psychiatric Advance Directive (PAD). This is a legal document that states your preferences in the event of a crisis. These may include your preferred representative if you lose insight or otherwise become incapacitated; a hospital setting, such as an intensive outpatient unit or inpatient unit; an alternative crisis setting, such as peer respite; various treatment options and medications.

Make sure the people treating you have your permission to communicate with your designated representative. A prior crisis can provide you with invaluable insights on what does and doesn't work for you in a crisis plan. It is important to know in advance whom to call if you experience a crisis, including your healthcare provider(s) or a crisis intervention team. This is a response team that includes mental health professionals.

You might be able to address the crisis without resorting to calling 911, which should be treated as a final option and can be emotionally distressing. In order to do so, it's crucial that you know the early warning signs that your condition may be deteriorating. Talk to your loved ones and healthcare providers about these signs and have an action plan in place if they occur. Let them know how they can help you if they notice these signs, and commit yourself to reaching out for help if you notice any of these signs yourself.

Let your prescriber know if you haven't been taking your medication consistently. Sometimes the most common reason for relapse is medication non-adherence. Your prescriber is there to help, not judge. Sometimes a medication adjustment is all it takes to help you in a crisis. Being ready can help reduce the chances of worst-case scenarios, such as (involuntary) hospitalization, which nobody wants. Planning ahead and acting early can save you the regret of a crisis.

EXERCISE

Start thinking about a crisis plan for yourself by answering the following questions:

- Who can help me prepare a crisis plan?

- What potential situations would I like to address and how would I like them to be addressed in my crisis plan?

- What are the early warning signs that I might need to implement my crisis plan?

- Do any of my loved ones know my early warning signs? Can I talk to them about my signs? (You may be concerned that this will cause them to worry or overreact – don't let these assumptions stop you from reaching out.)

- What would I like my loved ones to do if they observe any of my early warning signs?

- How severe should these early warning signs get before I/my loved ones should take action?

- Do I have a plan with my prescriber and non-prescriber to handle a crisis?

SELF-CARE

42

MONITOR YOURSELF

GOALS

Illness self-management is one of the best ways to ensure your continued positive mental health. You have a significant role to play in this. Staying well is so much more than seeing your therapist or psychiatrist on a regular schedule. You have to know how to take care of yourself in between your appointments.

Remember that your loved ones can also be a great help. Both you and your supporters need to understand everything that might impact your condition. Learn to recognize the way you feel when you're well – this is your "baseline." Then, monitor your moods and activities daily or weekly in a journal. Ensure you take note when your mood or behavior starts to change negatively, as this may be an early warning sign that you need help.

Consider what happened in past times of crisis and how you dealt with the situation then. Take a reputable online mental health screening such as the PHQ-2 for depression. You can also take a free Mental Health Screening at the website of Mental Health America (Mental Health America, n.d.). It is vital that you try to apply your coping strategies. If they don't work, you may need the help of a supporter or healthcare provider. It's important to recognize when you need help and know how to ask for it. In cases such as this, it's best not to delay too long or think something can wait until the next appointment. Acting now can make your situation far easier to address.

Listen to your supporters if they tell you they're concerned. Sometimes they can identify early signs of an episode sooner than you can. And have a plan with your caregiver to address concerns. Many situations can be easily addressed. For example, a quick medication adjustment might be all that you need. However, don't assume things will resolve themselves on their own, especially if they haven't in the past. It's critically important to know when you need help and ask for it. Proactively discussing your concerns with your doctor and monitoring your condition will not only help keep you well, but maximize the benefit you get from treatment.

EXERCISE

Periodically monitoring your moods and functions in relation to events and treatment can be helpful. There are various mood tracker apps you can try to help you with this. Tracking this yourself can also be easy with certain simple techniques. For example, you can periodically rank your mood on a scale of 1 (worst) to 10 (best).

The following considerations may help you make the most of this wellness practice over time.

- What is your baseline?

- Consider your baseline and what you're like on your best days, your worst days and the days that fall somewhere in between. If, at your baseline, you are normally a bit melancholic or engage in limited activity of one type, there may not be any cause for concern.

- Note your averages and when you are trending above or below these averages. Compare your observations to past experiences, as they can help you determine when there may be reason for concern.

- What events commonly have a negative impact on your baseline?

- What can you do to reduce the impact of adverse events?

43

SELF-CARE ESSENTIALS

GOALS

Self-care is taking good care of your emotional and physical health. The most important areas to maintain are good sleep, an active lifestyle, a healthy diet and positive support. Many self-care activities seek to better manage, prevent, eliminate, reduce, interrupt and cope with stress of varying intensities. These activities can be critical to good illness self-management.

Self-care strategies can be especially helpful in managing stress. Stress can trigger an illness or episode, worsen symptoms or make it harder to treat your illness. There are a wide range of internal sources of stress, such as difficulties with illness management and self-stigma. External sources of stress can be related to work, relationships and your environment (work and home).

Each person experiences their own stressors, but self-care activities can help manage a wide range of these. Good sleep can be the most important self-care activity. You may struggle with it. This is a key sign that you might be experiencing stress, which can worsen over time. As such, you must always do what you can to protect and improve your sleep.

Sometimes medication can also be helpful. You should watch out for the physical signs of stress, which may include frequent headaches and various aches and pains. Examples of emotional signs include anger, mood swings, difficultly concentrating and irritability. You can use self-care coping strategies to problem-solve a source of stress or develop coping strategies to minimize the emotional impact of stressful events.

An approach to stress management that considers the "whole you" is best. To most effectively manage stress, you need to turn self-care activities into habits and make them part of your day-to-day routine. This requires discipline. Small stressors should be addressed early, before they worsen and become more unmanageable. Try getting a self-care buddy to help keep you on track. Self-care can significantly support the medical treatment you receive – it should never be viewed as an option, but as a necessity.

EXERCISE

The following are strategies you can use to exercise self-care and improve your quality of life. Read through the list below and think about how you can incorporate them into your routine.

- **Sleep tips:** Aim to get 7 or more hours of sleep per night, wake up and go to bed at the same time daily, limit naps, do not eat or consume caffeine too late, create a relaxing sleep space and have a relaxing pre-bed routine (American Academy of Sleep Medicine, n.d.).
- **Exercise tips:** Aim to get at least 150 minutes of moderate-intensity aerobic physical activity each week. Your exercise routine should involve aerobic exercises such as walking, jogging or riding a bike, as well as muscle-strengthening exercises such as push-ups and sit-ups (Centers for Disease Control and Prevention, n.d.). Getting motivated can be hard, but over time you'll be able to do more, increase the intensity of your workouts and build endurance. If your budget allows it, working with a trainer can help.
- **Diet tips:** Focus on whole fruits; vary your veggies; make half your grains whole grains; vary your protein intake, such as seafood, lean meats, poultry, eggs, beans, peas, nuts and seeds; and move to low-fat or fat-free dairy milk or yogurt. Minimize consumption of saturated fats, trans fats, cholesterol, salt and added sugars (My Plate, US Department of Agriculture, n.d.).
- **Support tips:** Loneliness can be highly distressing and detrimental to both your mental and physical health. Try to develop a strong support network and don't be afraid to ask for help. Socialize with friends, family and community members as much as you can.

44

DAILY ACTIVITIES

GOALS

One cannot live on medication, therapy and the most essential activities of life alone. We need to be active and engaged every day – come rain or shine, happiness or sadness. Daily activities can add structure to your day, which can be critical to your recovery.

However, in order for these to be effective, you have to turn them into habits and make them part of your routine – take them seriously. There are many activities to choose from – some that will work well, some that won't, some that will work better when you're in a certain mood, some that you must do to stay well and some that you can choose to do for your own enjoyment. You may find that some activities are particularly helpful to your mental health, and may want to prioritize those.

It's always good to keep a schedule of recurring and planned activities. Ask your friends, family and healthcare providers for their recommendations. Read articles about self-care in reputable publications. Activities can positively impact the emotional, physical, spiritual and social aspects of your identity. They can help you relax, focus on the present moment and distract you from negative thoughts and rumination. Moreover, they can build your energy and endurance. However, remember that it's important to take breaks.

Moving forward, it's vital that you engage in activities that you enjoy, as that will make it more likely that you'll do them more regularly. Usually, the better you get at an activity, the more you will enjoy it, so it's best to try each new activity a few times before deciding whether it is or isn't right for you.

Make sure to select a good mix of activities to avoid boredom. Pick some you can do alone or with a friend, outdoors and indoors and when your energy is low or high. Self-care activities can give you a sense of achievement, help keep you healthy and give you the energy you'll need on your recovery journey.

EXERCISE

Keep doing what works for you, but always make sure to try new things. Below is a list of self-care activities for you to consider. Pick one or a few to try out. Come back to this list on a regular basis. Add your own ideas to the list and pick new ones to try each time.

Get out of bed	Write a gratitude list	Meet new people
Take a shower	Try gardening	Hug someone
Brush your teeth	Avoid social media	Spend time with family
Dress nicely	Turn off the TV	Spend time alone
Eat breakfast	Listen to music	Talk about your
Don't smoke	Read	emotions
Don't drink	Journal	Play with animals
Don't get upset	Try an adult coloring book	Play with children
Get outside	Try photography	Take a class
Go for a walk	Pray	Go shopping
Travel	Paint/draw	Go out for coffee
Stretch	Cook/bake	Go out for a meal
Breathe deeply	Knit/crochet	Take the day off
Meditate	Clean/organize	Do nothing
Smile / laugh	Socialize	Shorten your to-do list
Practice mindfulness	Text/call/Zoom a friend	

- Add your own self-care ideas below.

45

COMMITMENT

GOALS

Self-care can't work without commitment on your part. You have to try to be active whether you're feeling well or unwell. Remember that sometimes when you're feeling unwell is when you get the most out of practicing self-care. This can take a lot of willpower at times, and you may not feel like it at points, but it's worth it. What matters most is that you find out what works for you. Everyone is different.

Practice self-care at a comfortable pace – don't wear yourself out one day and do nothing the next day. Keep an activity schedule – maintaining structure in your daily life can be very effective in managing mental illness. Note the frequency of each activity, both the essential and the fun, as well as the intensity level required. Aim for low or moderate intensity levels on the days when you're not feeling as well.

By doing so regularly, you may come to associate certain activities with positive moods and learn to select activities that work best for your current mental state. Try to make the environment around you more conducive to self-care. You can do so by decluttering your home or joining a gym. Learn about the resources in your community such as free exercise classes. Find someone else who has the same objective as you and plan activities together, challenging one another to do better and comparing notes.

Sharing your goals with a loved one or on social media may increase your chances of working hard to meet them. Your supporters may also give you extra support to help you reach your goals. You have to avoid unnecessary temptations like buying junk food if you're trying to lose weight. Or, you can even try a behavioral economics technique called "loss aversion."

This involves giving a friend a sum of money and telling them they can keep it if you don't reach your goals. The risk of losing money may make you work harder.

Finally, when you accomplish something, celebrate it. Your journey to recovery will be much easier if you find ways to make it fun. Fun self-care is the best self-care.

EXERCISE

Make a list of self-care activities you like or want to do.

Keep your self-care list manageable. Don't overwhelm yourself or you may do a lot less. Know when to take breaks. Note the who, what, when, where and why for your daily and weekly activities. Challenge yourself and keep track of your progress and success.

Daily self-care activities:

Weekly self-care activities:

46

WELLNESS

GOALS

Health is about all of you, the whole person. This is what we mean by "wellness". "It is a conscious, deliberate process that requires being aware of and making choices for a more satisfying lifestyle" (Swarbick, 2006). This includes a sense of balance and fulfillment, and encompasses everything that makes recovery possible – in a way, it is recovery itself.

One framework for thinking about wellness is the "Eight Dimensions of Wellness" proposed by Dr. Swarbrick (Swarbick, 2006). This includes physical, intellectual, financial, environmental, spiritual, social, occupational and emotional wellness, all of which are interconnected and overlapping. For example, if you lose your job (occupational), you may become depressed (emotional), which may impact your relationships (social). This model of wellness focuses on strengths, with each aspect having the potential to positively or adversely impact your mental health.

There are many ways to improve your wellness, including numerous physical exercise options. Intellectual activities that can improve your wellness include reading and journaling. Meanwhile, good money-management skills can enhance your financial wellbeing. To learn more about this, you can try taking a personal finance course.

Spending time outside, especially walking, can improve your environmental wellness, while finding a spiritual connection through meditation, prayer or nature can help you cope with the uncertainties and daily stresses of life. You may be religious or spiritual – both may provide you with a sense of connectedness to something larger. Social connections, such as spending time with friends, family and community members are also critical to good mental health. Occupational stress is a leading stressor, so it's important to have a meaningful occupation and maintain a proper work/life balance.

We've already talked about many ways to address emotional wellness. Mental health challenges may make it hard to pursue overall wellness, but it's critical to your overall wellbeing. Feeling negative about one of these dimensions can negatively affect how you feel across the others. You can't let the other aspects of your life negatively impact your mental health. Sometimes this is unavoidable, but coping strategies can help.

Wellness is all about developing and maintaining balance, while managing the various aspects of your life. You need to find ways to motivate yourself to do what's best for your whole person. You can experience wellness even if you have a mental illness.

EXERCISE

As you go through this exercise, it can be helpful to examine each wellness dimension one-by-one.

- What activities are you currently doing that support your Eight Dimensions of Wellness?

  1. Physical wellness:

  2. Intellectual wellness:

  3. Financial wellness:

  4. Environmental wellness:

  5. Spiritual wellness:

  6. Social wellness:

  7. Occupational wellness:

  8. Emotional wellness:

- Which of your Eight Dimensions of Wellness need the most work to improve?

- What are some of the barriers you face in working to enhance your Eight Dimensions of Wellness? How can you remove these barriers?

47

COMPLEMENTARY HEALTH

GOALS

Many people use non-mainstream healthcare approaches. When these are used together with conventional medicine, it's considered "complementary." If a non-mainstream approach is used in place of mainstream medicine, it's considered "alternative." Most people who use non-mainstream approaches also use mainstream approaches. However, strictly alternative approaches to treating serious mental illness have not generally been acknowledged as effective replacements for traditional medicine.

Integrative health brings conventional and complementary approaches together in a coordinated way, emphasizing multimodal interventions. According to the National Center for Complementary and Integrative Medicine, the ten most popular complementary health approaches are: natural products, deep breathing, yoga, tai chi or qi gong, chiropractic or osteopathic manipulation, meditation, massage, special diets, homeopathy, progressive relaxation and guided imagery (National Center for Complementary and Integrative Medicine, n.d.). You should check with your doctor before you try these, as natural products may adversely impact your medication treatment or lead to significant side effects.

Meditation and deep breathing have been found to relieve anxiety and depression in some people (National Center for Complementary and Integrative Medicine, n.d.). There are some forms of meditation you can do alone and others that require groups. Many gyms and community centers offer classes. Group classes can be more motivating than trying to do them on your own. It's also a great way to meet new people.

Mindfulness meditation is a type of meditation in which a "person focuses attention on his or her breathing, and thoughts, feelings, and sensations are experienced freely as they arise" which increases awareness of the present moment. Evidence shows that mindfulness meditation can help reduce stress, anxiety and depression (Goyal, 2014). There's a reason that many people swear by it. Why not try it as an add on to your regular treatment, with the consultation of your healthcare provider? Think about it. If you believe it might be helpful, give it a try.

EXERCISE

- Which complementary health approaches do you think you might benefit from?

- What non-mainstream complementary health approaches can complement your mainstream approach?

- Where can you practice complementary health approaches?

RELATIONSHIPS

48

HELPFUL CAREGIVERS

GOALS

Caregivers can provide you with critical support. Most will want to help, but many may not know how. They may try their best, but they sometimes feel like nothing they do seems to help. This can leave them feeling frustrated, saddened, inadequate, powerless or hopeless. Sometimes they may simply lack knowledge or be misinformed.

Caregiving can be hard, and we don't always make things easy for our caregivers. We may be angry about having an illness and project that anger onto them. We may withdraw and isolate, pushing them away because we think we're a burden, but that can hurt them. We have to help them help us. We need to engage and collaborate with our caregivers. If there's silence between you and your caregiver, don't assume the worst – talk about it. Tell them your needs and wants, your sensitivities and triggers. If you don't, this may lead to misunderstandings and conflict, which can worsen your condition. Open, respectful, calm and honest dialogue and a trusting relationship are critical.

If your caregiver does something upsetting, give them the benefit of the doubt. If they offer advice, be open-minded and don't get defensive or be dismissive. Consider it. Also think about letting them participate in your treatment by giving them permission to speak with your healthcare provider(s). They often worry a lot about us. They want to make sure that we're getting the best treatment possible, but if we shut them out, they're left to wonder.

You may also want to preserve your privacy. This is your decision. Agreeing on a role for your caregiver to play in your treatment might help both of you. Always remember that you and your caregiver both have the same objective – to see you well. The most important supporter quality is that they never lose hope in you, even when you might.

EXERCISE

Rank your caregiver on the qualities below, assigning the following scores: 1 – have it, 2 – could be better, 3 – would be nice to have. Talk to them about how they are helping you and what they could do to be more helpful. You should also carry out a self-assessment to rank your own qualities.

Accepting	Non-judgmental
Allows me to be vulnerable	Patient
Asks me what helps	Reaches out to me
Believes my concerns	Reminds me of my strengths
Celebrates my successes	Respectful
Does things I enjoy	Respects my independence
Empathetic	Respects my privacy
Encourages me	Sensitive
Flexible	Tells me I'm important
Forgiving	Tells me they're proud of me
Good listener	Thoughtful
Honest	Trustworthy
Is there for me	Understanding
Lets me make decisions	Validates my feelings
Loving	Gives helpful feedback
Makes me feel good	Well-intentioned

49

GOOD COMMUNICATION

GOALS

Good communication is critical to healthy relationships. Talking about mental illness can be hard. It may lead to outbursts of frustration or impulsive and spontaneous remarks. Hurtful things may be said unintentionally. You may get defensive, justify your behaviors or deflect blame. Meanwhile, caregivers may do things they think will help you that might feel hurtful. For example, they may reward healthy behaviors, but withdraw support for self-destructive habits. They may accuse you of not trying hard enough, being lazy or using your illness as an excuse. This can be infuriating. However, as hard as it may be, you need to walk away from these arguments.

Try communicating with your supporters. A great way to start a conversation is by acknowledging a supporter's help and that being a caregiver can be hard, because it can be. Try to find a good time to talk. Avoid using an accusatory tone or criticizing them. Be calm and respectful. A few communication techniques you may find useful in such conversations are: restating and reflecting the other's persons point-of-view, summarizing, keeping the conversation flowing, asking for more details, describing feelings, politely giving feedback, validating concerns, pausing and avoiding conflict.

Another very effective communication technique is using "I" statements where you focus on the problem rather than the person. For example, "I feel upset when people call me lazy," instead of, "You make me upset when you call me lazy." The "I" approach lets you communicate your message without making the other person feel defensive. Apologizing for something unkind that you did can help mend relationships, relieve your guilt and make your bond stronger. These techniques can improve discussions.

Sometimes seeing a therapist together for a consultation or having a family meeting may help. SAMHSA's Evidence-Based Practice of Family Psychoeducation may be helpful here. Let your supporter know that you want your relationship to be better. Open dialogue is the best way to work together to overcome some of the challenges of living with mental illness. Shutting down communication rarely works.

EXERCISE

Does you supporter exhibit any of the negative behaviors below toward you? Circle any behaviors below that you think apply to your supporter. Talk to them about your concerns without being critical, judgmental or argumentative.

Judges and criticizes me	Stone-walls me
Says hurtful things to me	Is possessive
Offers unsolicited advice	Blames me
Exhibits controlling behaviors	Nags me
Ignores my concerns	Guilt-trips me
Dismisses my concerns	Questions my judgment
Diminishes my concerns	Does not trust me
Minimizes my feelings	Does not respect by privacy
Triggers me	Interferes with my relationships
Manipulates me	Has unrealistic expectations for me
Threatens me	
	Disrespects my boundaries
Threatens to abandon me	
	Gets frustrated with me
Punishes or threatens to punish me	
	Is unwilling to compromise
Intimidates me	Gaslights me

50

FRIENDSHIPS

GOALS

Friendships are as important to people with mental illness as anyone else. In fact, mental illness may show us the friends that truly care. They will express concern when you don't seem well, ask you how you're doing, respond to your messages in a reasonable time and check in on you. Some friends may not know what to say to you and may worry that they might say something insensitive or hurtful. Reach out to them and let them know that their friendship is important to you. Make sure to tell them that you understand if they find it difficult to talk about your illness, but you know they care nonetheless. This may make them feel more comfortable.

Sometimes we may need to repair a friendship if we've said or done something hurtful, like push someone away. Reach out to them. Have an open discussion, avoid blame and apologize if it's appropriate. Talking about good memories can remind you both of the strength of your relationship. Importantly, don't force it – time can be the best healer. Sadly, it's not uncommon for us to lose some friends when we become sick. A major reason for this is stigma – this is on them, not you.

Some people don't want to be friends with someone with a mental illness – this is their loss, and it is important to understand that these friends aren't worth keeping, even if it is painful to realize this. Look for signs. Do you feel anxious before seeing them or exhausted afterwards? Do you feel like you're walking on eggshells around them, that you're insecure about your relationship or that you lack trust in them? These are all things to watch for. We can't stay in bad relationships just because we're afraid of being alone.

Not all friendships are made to last. It is important to value the quality of friendships over the quantity. Cherish your friends, let them in, be a good friend to them and a good friend to yourself.

EXERCISE

- Make a list of old friendships you would like to strengthen or repair.

  1.

  2.

  3.

  4.

  5.

  6.

  7.

  8.

  9.

  10.

- Scratch anyone off the list who you think might not understand how mental illness affected your behaviors in the past.
- For the remaining names, make a specific plan for how you will try to reconnect with them.

51

BOUNDARIES

GOALS

Boundaries are all about you. Establishing boundaries means setting limits on the behaviors of others toward you. It means prioritizing yourself. Effective boundaries can help you boost your self-esteem and self-worth, make you feel empowered and help you avoid discomfort, triggering behavior and resentment.

Vitally, they can help you create, strengthen and preserve healthy relationships. All of these things are good for your mental health. Some examples of boundaries include: taking breaks and time off from relationships, saying no and not needing to explain or prove yourself to anyone and not pleasing everyone all the time.

You're allowed to listen to and act on your feelings by disengaging from conversations and people, protecting your energy, valuing your time, creating safe places and sharing how you really feel. Be willing to negotiate your boundaries, state consequences for disrespecting them and be ready to enforce those consequences.

You may be afraid that people will not like you, or that they will reject or abandon you. This may be a bit uncomfortable, but pay close attention to those who become angry. Some people may even try to gaslight you, which is when someone manipulates you into questioning your own reality. All of these can be unhelpful and hurtful.

Sometimes it may become necessary to end some relationships. Be sure to resist the urge to apologize and remove boundaries unless you feel you acted too rashly or made a mistake. Gut instincts can be strong indicators of what you really want and need. Don't feel guilty about acting on them. If the person truly cares about you, they'll respect your desire to set boundaries and will try not to overstep them. You should also respect the boundaries others may place on you, including how much support they can offer you and when. Setting boundaries is an act of self-love. Sometimes saying no to others allows you to say yes to yourself.

EXERCISE

Pick a good time and place to have a discussion about boundaries. Try to make this a calm and respectful conversation. Below are a few examples of how you could express simple boundaries with your friends or family:

- I won't be able to make it, but thank you for the invitation.
- I'd love to help you, but I'm not at my best right now.
- Thank you for that suggestion, but I don't think it's right for me.
- Thank you for your concern, but please don't check in on me so often.
- I want you to be involved in my care, but if you "____" again, "____."
- I know it's important, but I don't feel like talking about it right now.
- I don't like it when you talk to me that way. If you do, I won't be able to spend time with you.

What are some boundaries you'd like to set? Be specific. Think of the who, what, where, when, and why of each one.

1.

2.

3.

4.

5.

52

SOCIALIZATION

GOALS

Socializing may be difficult, but it can be very helpful to good mental health. You may fear stigma, judgment, lack of empathy and rejection. Perhaps you believe others may not like you if they knew you had an illness. You may be ashamed and embarrassed to see people because you think that they may be able to tell you're not well. In order to maintain friendships, you might feel like you have to "fake it," which may make you feel dishonest, resentful, awkward or uncomfortable.

You may judge others unfairly when you make unfounded assumptions that they'll stigmatize you. You might fear that spending time with an old friend might remind you of happier times you think will not return. All of this may make you isolate and withdraw. This is very bad for your mental health.

Remember that there are techniques you can use to make socializing a little more comfortable. For example, you can pick a "safe" setting for your meetings with friends. Try to come prepared to answer uncomfortable questions like, "How are you doing?" Know how to change the topic – say, for example, "Maybe we can talk about that later." Only share what you feel comfortable sharing, and have an exit plan ready if things get uncomfortable.

Don't self-sabotage relationships by pushing people away because you assume they'll eventually abandon you. Instead, try to guide those who seem a bit uncomfortable talking about mental illness. Try not to avoid people you care about because you are worried they may think you don't like them. By doing so, you may be losing out on important care and support.

You have to get out there, step outside your home, meet with old friends and make new ones through activities and events. We can't live our lives alone, and being around others can make us happy. Remember, many people want to spend time with someone just like you.

EXERCISE

- Who are your most important friends?

- Which of your important friends have you not told about your illness? What are the pros and cons of not telling them now?

- What can you do to strengthen your relationships?

- If someone asks how you're feeling, and you're not feeling well, how would you answer? You could respond: "Thank you for asking"; "Not so great today"; "A little down"; or, "I appreciate your concern."

- If someone asks what you do and you're unemployed, try answering: "I am not working right now"; "I am taking some time off"; or, "I'm working on personal growth."

53

PEER SUPPORT

GOALS

Peer support is when people use shared experiences to help each other. There's strong evidence that this works. In fact, it can be invaluable. Seeing just one example of someone like you in recovery can inspire you to believe that recovery is possible.

Peers can also help combat loneliness and isolation – just knowing that they're out there, even if they're not by your side, can make you feel less alone. You can motivate and help one another by sharing hopes, struggles, successes, insights and coping strategies. This can help reduce some of the uncertainty you may be feeling about your journey to recovery.

The empathy bond formed between peers can be strong. A peer can more easily than others recognize, understand and celebrate your successes, as well as the difficulties of setbacks and disappointments. Peers can receive and give help, care and be cared for, empower and self-empower.

A peer may inspire you when you're struggling, setting you on the path toward recovery and getting you back on track when you've gone astray. Peers can boost your self-esteem and self-worth and make you feel needed. The best way to find peers is to speak to friends and family. You may learn that you know people who struggle too.

Moreover, you can find peers in support groups, Clubhouses and through volunteer work for mental health non-profits. You can even find some online at ForLikeMinds.com, other online peer support communities and mental health-focused social media pages like the ForLikeMinds Facebook page. Certified Peer Specialists ("CPSs") are another great resource. They are people living with mental illness in recovery trained to deliver peer support to help those who are struggling (National Association of Peer Supporters, 2023). They make invaluable contributions to our community. In fact, it is highly likely that most people living with mental illness could benefit from the support of CPSs. In the end, nobody understands your mental illness better than your peers. Speaking with peers will also give you the opportunity to share your own insights and offer support. This can give you the wonderful feeling of helping someone just like you to overcome their struggles.

EXERCISE

Look into whether there is a Clubhouse in your local area such as Fountain House. Clubhouses provide a model of psychiatric rehabilitation which offers socialization opportunities for people living with mental illness while addressing daily living needs. The National Alliance on Mental Illness (NAMI) (Duckworth, 2022) also offers an educational program called Peer-to-Peer that provides opportunities for mutual growth and support. This program is offered across the country at local affiliates such as NAMI-NYC.

Start thinking about peers that may be helpful in your recovery journey by answering the following questions. Remember that your lived experience may help them too over time.

- Do I know anyone living with mental illness?

- What family members or friends can I talk to about finding peers?

- Which in-person peer support groups can I contact to connect with peers?

- Which online peer support groups can I contact to connect with peers?

- Where else can I find peers?

54

EMOTIONAL SUPPORT ANIMALS

GOALS

Pets or emotional support animals (ESAs) can be a tremendous source of support – so much so that they are often considered family members. At times, they can even be more supportive than your human relatives. Animal companions can help reduce stress, depression, anxiety, loneliness and isolation, as well as providing unconditional support, creating a calming presence and diverting negative thoughts. They can help improve your overall quality of life by providing owners with a sense of responsibility, purpose and accomplishment, encouraging exercise, offering socialization opportunities and adding structure and routine to your daily life.

Pets can make you laugh or show affection as if intuitively knowing when you may need a little extra support. Many people like to speak to their pets, because they don't fear judgment or feel like a burden. For those of us in the depths of despair, they are one of many reasons to live. You may wonder who will take care of them if you weren't around.

Many animals can qualify to be an ESA. Some common ESAs are dogs, cats, rabbits and hamsters. Equine (horse) therapy has been shown to be effective (WebMD, 2021). For an animal to qualify as an ESA, you'll need a letter from a healthcare provider or agency stating that you can benefit emotionally from them. Many local laws accord people with an ESA special privileges, such as the ability to reside in a no-pet building with an ESA and travel with an ESA in an airline cabin. A service dog has even more rights and privileges, but they can be very costly. Service dogs have been shown to be especially effective for people who suffer from PTSD, such as veterans.

You should only consider getting an animal companion if you're truly committed to taking care of it. Remember, you need love and support, and they do too!

EXERCISE

- Have you considered pet sitting, visiting a dog park or fostering a pet?

- Have you thought of volunteering at an animal shelter?

- Who can you talk to about picking the best animal for you and what questions would you ask them? For example, you might want to talk about breed, caring, training, etc.

- What do you think a pet can help you with?

- Do you have the time and space to properly take care of a pet?

FINAL WORDS

Congratulations! You made it to the end. I hope that, over the course of this workbook, you've gained valuable skills, your confidence has grown and you've realized that recovery may indeed be possible for you.

Most of all, I hope you've found a little hope that will carry you along this never-ending journey called recovery.

Dare to dream of the life you want and work as hard as you can to reach it, because you deserve to feel better.

Know that you'll never be alone on this journey. You will be in the thoughts and hearts of your peers and the many people who need you, care for you and love you.

I believe in you. You have to believe in you too.

Safe journeys.

"The journey of a thousand miles begins with one step."

—Lao Tzu

REFERENCES

American Academy of Sleep Medicine, AASM, Sleep Education. (n.d.) *Healthy Sleep*. Retrieved March 19, 2023 from https://sleepeducation.org/healthy-sleep/

American Foundation for Suicide Prevention (n.d.). *Risk factors, protective factors, and warning signs.* Retrieved March 19, 2023 from https://afsp.org/risk-factors-protective-factors-and-warning-signs

American Psychological Association (2010). *Psychodynamic Psychotherapy Brings Lasting Benefits through Self-Knowledge.* Retrieved March 19, 2023 from https://www.apa.org/news/press/releases/2010/01/psychodynamic-therapy#:~:text=Psychodynamic%20therapy%20focuses%20on%20the,patterns%20in%20the%20patient's%20life

Anthony, W. (1993). "Recovery from mental illness: the guiding vision of the mental health system in the 1990s", *Psychosocial Rehabilitation Journal*, 16(4), 11-23.

Beck, A.T. (1963). "Thinking and depression: Idiosyncratic content and cognitive distortions" *Archives of General Psychiatry*, 9(4), 324-333

Beck Institute. (n.d.). *Understanding CBT.* Retrieved March 19, 2023 from https://beckinstitute.org/about/understanding-cbt/#:~:text=Cognitive%20Behavior%20Therapy%20helps%20people,problems%20and%20initiating%20behavioral%20changes.

Beck, J. (2021) "Cognitive Behavior Therapy: Basics and Beyond" (3rd Edition). New York: Guilford.

Behavioral Tech (Dialectical Behavioral Therapy) (n.d.). Retrieved March 19, 2023 from https://behavioraltech.org/

Bellamy, C. *et al.* (2017). "An update on the growing evidence base for peer support," *Mental Health and Social Inclusion.*

Bolles, N. Richard *et al.* (2021). "What Color Is Your Parachute? Job-Hunter's Workbook" (6th Ed.), Ten Speed Press, Berkeley.

Centers for Disease Control and Prevention (CDC) (n.d.). *How much physical activity do adults need?* Retrieved March 19, 2023 from https://www.cdc.gov/physicalactivity/basics/adults/index.htm

Chinman M. *et al.* (2014). "Peer Support Services for Individuals With Serious Mental Illnesses: Assessing the Evidence," *Psychiatric Services.*

Corrigan, P. (2004). "How Stigma Interferes With Mental Health Care." *American Psychologist*, 59 (7), 614-625.

Davidson, L. & Strauss, J.S. (1992). "Sense of self in recovery from severe mental illness". *British Journal of Medical Psychology*, 65, 131-145.

Duckworth, K. (2022). "You are Not Alone: The NAMI Guide to Navigating Mental Health With Advice from Experts and Wisdom from Real People and Families." Zando.

Drucker, P. F. (1954). "The practice of management." New York, NY: HarperCollins.

Fredrickson, B. (2004) "The broaden-and-build theory of positive emotions". *Philos Trans R Soc Lond B Biol Sci.*, 359(1449): 1367–1378.

Fromm, E. (1956). "The Art of Living," Harper and Row.

Goyal M. *et al.* (2014) "Meditation Programs for Psychological Stress and Well-being," *JAMA Internal Medicine.*

Mental Health America. (n.d.) *Take a Mental Health Test.* Retrieved March 19, 2023 from https://screening.mhanational.org/screening-tools/

Miller, W. R., & Rollnick, S. (2013). "Motivational interviewing: Helping people change" (3rd ed.). New York, NY: Guilford Press.

My Plate, US Department of Agriculture. Retrieved March 19, 2023 from https://www.myplate.gov/eat-healthy/what-is-myplate

National Association of Peer Supporters (2023). "What it Takes: Wisdom from Peer Support Specialists and Supervisors", Independently Published.

National Alliance on Mental Illness (n.d.). *Mental Health by the Numbers.* Retrieved March 19, 2023 from https://www.nami.org/mhstats

National Center for Complementary and Integrative Health. (n.d.). *Meditation and Mindfulness: What You Need to Know).* Retrieved March 19, 2023 from https://www.nccih.nih.gov/health/meditation-and-mindfulness-what-you-need-to-know#:~:text=Meditation%20and%20mindfulness%20practices%20may,nicotine%2C%20alcohol%2C%20or%20opioids.

National Institute of Mental Health, (n.d.). *Mental Illness.* Retrieved March 19, 2023 from https://www.nimh.nih.gov/health/statistics/mental-illness

Prochaska, J. (1983). "Stages of change in psychotherapy: Measurement and sample profiles." *Psychotherapy: Theory, Research & Practice, 20*(3), 368–375.

Ritsher, J. *et al.* (2003). "Internalized Stigma Mental Illness Inventory-19; Internalized stigma of mental illness: psychometric properties of a new measure." *Psychiatry Res.,* 31-49.

Rosenberg, M. (1965). "Rosenberg Self-Esteem Scale (RSES)" *APA PsycTests.*

SAMHSA (Substance Abuse and Mental Health Services Administration). (n.d.). *Family Psychoeducation (FPE) Evidenced-Based Practices Kit.* Retrieved March 19, 2023 from https://store.samhsa.gov/product/Family-Psychoeducation-Evidence-Based-Practices-EBP-KIT/SMA09-4422

SAMHSA (Substance Abuse and Mental Health Services Administration). (n.d.). *The FindTreatment.gov.* Retrieved March 19, 2023 from https://findtreatment.gov/

SAMHSA (Substance Abuse and Mental Health Services Administration). (n.d.). *Integrated Treatment for Co-occurring Disorders (ITCD) Evidenced-Based Practices Kit.* Retrieved March 19, 2023 from https://store.samhsa.gov/product/Integrated-Treatment-for-Co-Occurring-Disorders-Evidence-Based-Practices-EBP-KIT/SMA08-4366

SAMHSA (Substance Abuse and Mental Health Services Administration). (n.d.). *Permanent Supportive Housing Evidence-Based Practices Kit.* Retrieved March 19, 2023 from https://store.samhsa.gov/product/Permanent-Supportive-Housing-Evidence-Based-Practices-EBP-KIT/SMA10-4509

SAMHSA (Substance Abuse and Mental Health Services Administration). (n.d.). *Supported Education Evidence-Based Practices (EBP) KIT.* Retrieved March 19, 2023 from https://store.samhsa.gov/product/Supported-Education-Evidence-Based-Practices-EBP-KIT/SMA11-4654

SAMHSA (Substance Abuse and Mental Health Services Administration). (n.d.). *Supported Employment Evidence-Based Practices (EBP) Kit.* Retrieved March 19, 2023 from https://store.samhsa.gov/product/Supported-Employment-Evidence-Based-Practices-EBP-Kit/SMA08-4364

Swarbrick, M. (2006). "A Wellness Approach." *Psychiatric Rehabilitation Journal, 29*(4), 311-314.

Tedeschi, R. and Calhoun, L. (2009) "Posttraumatic Growth: Conceptual Foundations and Empirical Evidence", *An International Journal for the Advancement of Psychological Theory,* 15(1), 1-18.

US Department of Justice, Civil Rights Division. *American with Disabilities Act* of 1990, Title I and Title II Accommodations. (n.d.). Retrieved March 19, 2023 from https://www.dol.gov/agencies/odep/program-areas/employers/accommodations

US Department of Justice, Civil Rights Division, Section 504, *Rehabilitation Act* of 1973, Protecting Students with Disabilities. (n.d.). Retrieved March 19, 2023 from https://www2.ed.gov/about/offices/list/ocr/504faq.html

REFERENCES

VIA Institute on Character, (n.d.). *The 24 Character Strengths.* Retrieved March 19, 2023 from https://www.viacharacter.org/character-strengths

Warren, E. *et al.* (2005). "All Your Worth: The Ultimate Lifetime Money Plan." Free Press.

WebMD, "What is Equine Therapy and Equine-Assisted Therapy", April 9, 2021. Retrieved March 19, 2023 from https://www.webmd.com/mental-health/what-is-equine-therapy-equine-assisted-therapy

US MENTAL HEALTH
NON-PROFITS

Active Minds | Advocacy Unlimited | American Foundation for Suicide Prevention | Anxiety and Depression Association of America | Bazelon Center for Mental Health Law | Black Emotional and Mental Health Collective | Bring Change 2 Mind | Buddy Project | Child Mind Institute | Compassionate Friends | Crisis Text Line | Depressed Black Gay Men |Depression and Bipolar Support Alliance | Eating Disorders Information Network | Faces and Voices of Recovery | Fountain House | Gateway to Post Traumatic Stress Disorder Information | HeadsUpGuys | Healthy Minds Network | iFred | International Bipolar Foundation | International OCD Foundation | IntrusiveThoughts | Jed Foundation | The Kennedy Forum | Letters Against Depression | Live Through This | Man Therapy | Mental Health America | Mental Health Channel | Mental Health First Aid | Mental Health Gov | The Mighty | Military with PTSD | Mood Disorders Support Group | Mood Network | NADD | National Alliance on Mental Illness | National Alliance on Mental Illness Affiliates | National Association for Rights Protection and Advocacy | National Council for Behavioral Health | National Disability Rights Network | The National Eating Disorders Association | National Empowerment Center | National Federation of Families for Children's Mental Health | National Institute of Mental Health | National Mental Health Consumers' Self-Help Clearinghouse | National Resource Center for Hispanic Mental Health | National Suicide Prevention Lifeline | Now Matters Now | Objective Zero | PFLAG – Parents, Families, and Friends of Lesbians and Gays | Project Heal | Project UROK | Project Semicolon | SAMSHA – Substance Abuse and Mental Health Services Administration | Schizophrenia and Related Disorders Alliance of America | Shatterproof | Speaking of Suicide | The Stability Network | Stigma Fighters | Stop Soldier Suicide | Suicide Awareness Voices of Education | This is My Brave | Thunderbird Partnership Foundation | The Treatment Advocacy Center | The Trevor Project | Ulifeline | Warm Lines | Wounded Warrior Project | and many more.

CANADIAN MENTAL HEALTH NON-PROFITS

Anxiety Disorders Association of Canada | Bell Let's Talk | Canada Drug Rehab Addiction Services Directory | Canadian Association for Suicide Prevention | Canadian Mental Health Association | Centre for Suicide Prevention | Crisis Services Canada | Defeat Depression| Depression Hurts | First Nations and Inuit Hope for Wellness Help Line | Gerstein Crisis Centre | Good2Talk | Healthy Minds Cooperative | Mental Health Commission of Canada | Mind Your Mind | Mood Disorders Society of Canada | National Eating Disorder Information Centre | National Mental Health Inclusion Network | Schizophrenia Society of Canada | and many more.

MENTAL HEALTH RESOURCES

US

HelpGuide: www.helpguide.org

Mentalhealth.gov: www.mentalhealth.gov

Mental Health America: www.mhanational.org

National Alliance on Mental Illness (NAMI): www.nami.org

National Institute of Mental Health: www.nimh.nih.gov

Very Well Mind: www.verywellmind.com

Canada

Canadian Mental Health Association: cmha.ca

Crisis Service Canada: www.ementalhealth.ca

UK

Mental Health Foundation UK: www.mentalhealth.org.uk

Mind UK: www.mind.org.uk

Rethink Mental Illness: www.rethink.org

Samaritans: www.samaritans.org, helpline: 116 123

Scottish Association for Mental Health (SAMH): www.samh.org.uk

Shout: www.giveusashout.org, text 85258

Young Minds: www.youngminds.org.uk

Europe

Mental Health Europe: www.mhe-sme.org

Mental Health Ireland: www.mentalhealthireland.ie

Australia and New Zealand

Beyond Blue: www.beyondblue.org.au

Head to Health: headtohealth.gov.au

Health Direct: www.healthdirect.gov.au

Mental Health Australia: mhaustralia.org

Mental Health Foundation of New Zealand: www.mentalhealth.org.nz
SANE Australia: www.sane.org

SUPPORT FOR SUICIDAL THOUGHTS

If you are finding it difficult to cope or know someone who is, and need to be heard without judgment or pressure, you can find information and support from the following:

Crisis Text Line (US, Canada, UK, Ireland): www.crisistextline.org, text "HOME" to 741741 (US), "CONNECT" to 686868 (Canada), "SHOUT" to 85258 (UK), or "HOME" to 50808 (Ireland)

US

American Foundation for Suicide Prevention: afsp.org
National Suicide Prevention Lifeline: suicidepreventionlifeline.org, helpline: 988

Canada

Talk Suicide Canada: talksuicide.ca, helpline: 1 833 456 4566

UK

Campaign Against Living Miserably (CALM): www.thecalmzone.net, helpline: 0800 58 58 58
PAPYRUS (dedicated to the prevention of young suicide): www.papyrus-uk. org, helpline: 0800 068 4141
The Samaritans: www.samaritans.org, helpline: 116 123

Australia and New Zealand

Lifeline Australia: www.lifeline.org.au, helpline: 13 11 14
Lifeline New Zealand: www.lifeline.org.nz, helpline: 0800 543 354

TriggerHub.org is one of the most elite and scientifically proven forms of mental health intervention

Trigger Publishing is the leading independent mental health and wellbeing publisher in the UK and US. Our collection of bibliotherapeutic books and the power of lived experience change lives forever. Our courageous authors' lived experiences and the power of their stories are scientifically endorsed by independent federal, state and privately funded research in the US. These stories are intrinsic elements in reducing stigma, making those with poor mental health feel less alone, giving them the privacy they need to heal, ensuring they are guided by the essential steps to kick-start their own journeys to recovery, and providing hope and inspiration when they need it most.

Clinical and scientific research conducted by assistant professor Dr Kristin Kosyluk and her highly acclaimed team in the Department of Mental Health Law & Policy at the University of South Florida (USF), as well as complementary research by her peers across the US, has independently verified the power of lived experience as a core component in achieving mental health prosperity. Their findings categorically confirm lived experience as a leading method in treating those struggling with poor mental health by significantly reducing stigma and the time it takes for them to seek help, self-help or signposting if they are struggling.

Delivered through TriggerHub, our unique online portal and smartphone app, we make our library of bibliotherapeutic titles and other vital resources accessible to individuals and organizations anywhere, at any time and with complete privacy, a crucial element of recovery. As such, TriggerHub is the primary recommendation across the UK and US for the delivery of lived experiences.

At Trigger Publishing and TriggerHub, we proudly lead the way in making the unseen become seen. We are dedicated to humanizing mental health, breaking stigma and challenging outdated societal values to create real action and impact. Find out more about our world-leading work with lived experience and bibliotherapy via triggerhub.org, or by joining us on:

- 🐦 @triggerhub_
- 🅕 @triggerhub.org
- 📷 @triggerhub_

Dr Kristin Kosyluk, Ph.D., is an assistant professor in the Department of Mental Health Law and Policy at USF, a faculty affiliate of the Louis de la Parte Florida Mental Health Institute, and director of the STigma Action Research (STAR) Lab. Find out more about Dr Kristin Kosyluk, her team and their work by visiting:

USF Department of Mental Health Law & Policy:
www.usf.edu/cbcs/mhlp/index.aspx

USF College of Behavioral and Community Sciences:
www.usf.edu/cbcs/index.aspx

STAR Lab: www.usf.edu/cbcs/mhlp/centers/star-lab/

For more information, visit BJ-Super7.com

Printed in the USA
CPSIA information can be obtained
at www.ICGtesting.com
JSHW012017140824
68134JS00026B/2471